Finding the Raga

ALSO BY AMIT CHAUDHURI

Fiction
A Strange and Sublime Address
Afternoon Raag
Freedom Song
A New World
Real Time
The Immortals
Odysseus Abroad
Friend of My Youth

Nonfiction
Clearing a Space: Reflections on India, Literature, and Culture
Calcutta: Two Years in the City
Telling Tales: Selected Writing 1993–2013
The Origins of Dislike

As Editor
The Picador Book of Modern Indian Literature
Memory's Gold: Writings on Calcutta
Literary Activism: A Symposium

Poetry
St Cyril Road and Other Poems
Sweet Shop

Finding the Raga

An Improvisation on Indian Music

AMIT CHAUDHURI

nyrb **New York Review Books** New York

This is a New York Review Book

published by The New York Review of Books

435 Hudson Street, New York, NY 10014

www.nyrb.com

LIBRARY OF CONGRESS CATALOGING-IN-PUBLICATION DATA
Names: Chaudhuri, Amit, 1962– author.
Title: Finding the raga : an improvisation on Indian music / by Amit
 Chaudhuri.
Description: New York City : New York Review Books, 2020. |
 Identifiers: LCCN 2020016137 (print) | LCCN 2020016138 (ebook) |
 ISBN 9781681374789 (paperback) | ISBN 9781681374796 (ebook)
Subjects: LCSH: Music—India—Philosophy and aesthetics. | Raga. |
 Music and literature—India.
Classification: LCC ML3877 .C557 2020 (print) | LCC ML3877
 (ebook) | DDC 780.9/54—dc23
LC record available at https://lccn.loc.gov/2020016137
LC ebook record available at https://lccn.loc.gov/2020016138

ISBN 978-1-68137-478-9
Available as an electronic book; 978-1-68137-479-6

Printed in the United States of America on acid-free paper.

1 3 5 7 9 10 8 6 4 2

The seven notes of Indian music have been transcribed in the text in this way:

sa re ga ma pa dha ni

The higher octave (taar saptak) is shown in bold, the lower octave (mandra saptak) in italics:

sa re ga ma pa dha ni sa re ga ma pa dha ni
sa re ga ma pa dha ni

Flat notes are underlined: e.g. <u>dha</u> <u>ni</u>. Sharp notes are represented in this way: má.

Q: Can't art be born from happiness?

Kishori Amonkar: Of course it can. Why shouldn't it be?

Q: But you said *pain* and *suffering* lead to the *highest art.*

A: Because . . . life to us . . . I mean . . . Why don't you tell me: who is happy? [Silence.] Everyone is unhappy. By 'unhappy' one means the desire to return to where we came from. And from where we came – we call that place ananda [joy; bliss]. Our task is to take people to that ananda, by whatever means – whether through art or the shastras. That's what our life returns us to – and that's where it will take us to. If we don't go there, life will take us there anyway. But that's where it will go – to where we came from. *It is a completion of a circle.*

Q: *What are you searching for in your music?*

A: *I'm searching for that bliss! And not only me – I feel like giving that bliss to my listeners, to everybody. Everybody.*

Q: *What is that bliss?*

A: If you now ask me what ananda is, I won't be able to tell you. It's something you experience.

(Interview in Hindi and English with
Kishori Amonkar, 1991. English in italics.)

1
Alaap

That was a time of unsettlement. My father was pro-
moted after some uncertainty. He took charge of his
company. I always said 'his company' as one might say
'his town' when mentioning a place a friend belongs to.

To mark our new life, we moved flats. We came to
a four-bedroom flat with a study in Cuffe Parade, the
result of joining two flats on the top storey together. We
looked out on the Marine Drive and the sea from the
opposite side of where we'd lived for ten years. I could
see, from the balcony adjoining the drawing room, the
building I'd grown up in.

I think I was sixteen. I was acutely unhappy. We seemed
to have moved a great distance.

I remember sitting in the drawing room that first evening.
I didn't know where my parents were. I sat, semi-visible,
on a sofa. I was like an employee who finds he's out of
a job. I had delayed my arrival for as long as I could,
and now found myself in a vacuum I was told was my
'home', feeling no sense of homecoming.

The flat was coming into being. Things were being

unloaded and fitted. The twenty-five-storey building was in the last stages of completion.

On the other side of the water, I could see, if I focused, the past's outline.

Cuffe Parade was where it came to me that I had no real home – that habitation for me consisted of people: primarily my parents. I was where they happened to be.

I was no longer in school. I was in 'Junior College'. I went every other day to Elphinstone College to attend classes. I used to play the guitar and had begun to write songs, in keeping with Neil Young and Bob Dylan (whom I secretly didn't much care for). In the manner of most phases in pop history, that era seemed over almost as soon as it had begun, and I, who had never been to America, found myself caught on its outer edge, perhaps unaware that my moment – as a singer-songwriter – had passed, possibly unwilling to let it go. Among the things that were distracting me just then, in the midst of my virginal exploration of what it meant to be a songwriter, was Hindustani classical music.

I had heard – or overheard – Indian classical music as a child. A man or woman would be singing on the radio. The singing was instantly up for parody. I never dreamed then that I'd have anything to do with this tradition. My incredulous dismissal is, in its own way, a happy memory, to do with an interlude when I was

4

unconnected to what would consume me a decade later. Dismissal, in fact, is the default response to khayal (the pre-eminent genre of North Indian classical music), well before we get to know what khayal is, and vaguely term its strangeness 'classical music'. Those who later become acquainted with its extraordinary melodiousness forget that on the initial encounter it had sounded unmelodious. There may be many reasons for this first misprision. When I was growing up, it may have had to do with the fact that all kinds, old and young, talented and less talented, got periodic slots to sing on All India Radio once they'd passed an audition. How did they pass the audition if they didn't sing well? A singer of what are called 'light classical' forms in India would reply – Because pure classical music relegates tone and beauty to secondary status, or gives them no status at all, and privileges mastery of grammar. This is not quite true, but has enough truth to explain why people with voices that aren't musical sing khayal with authority. It's related to a Brahminical mode that Indian thinking is often in danger of slipping into.

Another reason might be that various forms of classical music pursue tonality to an extremity. Once the ear becomes used to the extremity, it hears beauty. The convergence between extremity and beauty particularly applies to the most sensuous vehicle of melody, the human voice. Whether singing opera or the khayal, the voice

– in very different ways – will seem far removed from its normal range and function, encroaching on registers that sound unnatural: so that it might provoke laughter, or cause impatience. Classical music might comprise one's heritage, but it also has an air of deep foreignness. Music was one facet of Indian culture that – for instance – the English coloniser simply didn't understand, and didn't care to. But Indian classical music is as incomprehensible to most Indians as it was to the English. One assumes the air of foreignness marks European classical forms too, not only for people from countries outside Europe. As far as alienated *Indian* responses to *Western* classical music are concerned, two come randomly to mind. The first is from my mother. She once told me that when she first heard strains of Western classical music, when living in London with my father in the fifties, they made her profoundly sad. Then there's Rabindranath Tagore, in his memoir *Jiban Smriti* ('My Reminiscences'), speaking about his time in London between 1878 and 1880. A woman singing reminds him of a horse neighing. The piano is an inferior instrument, because it can't execute glissandos; the violin is preferable. Of course, Tagore's remarks arise partly from politics and colonial tension. They mask a shrewd and creative interest in Western music common to many Indian composers.

There may be another reason why my aversion to Indian classical music turned to devotion. It has to do with the unpredictability of our lives as readers and writers, listeners and musicians. What's bored us might begin to obsess us. What seemed important might, one day, lose its interest. You can't be prepared by education, say, for Indian classical music. A change of direction may occur without warning. You find a point of entry you hadn't been looking for. This might also happen with a book. The book could be a canonical one. You read three pages, and it does nothing for you. A year later, you pick it up and read to the fourth page. It does nothing. One day, you read it determinedly, without pleasure, and, on page one hundred and twenty-five, you're struck by a phrase or simile; it unlocks the book's language and teaches you how to read it. The point of entry comes unawares; it makes a world or work available which you'd had no time for previously.

Until 1977 (when I finished school), I wanted to be a pop, then a rock, musician. My parents, probably thinking I'd become a chartered accountant, allowed me this fantasy. My father, an extraordinarily kind man, sponsored my enthusiasms. As a result, I possessed a Yamaha acoustic guitar with a sweet, expansive sound, and an Ibanez – both procured from Denmark Street on trips to London.

In 1978, I left school, and my anomalous side found play. I turned into a quasi-modernist. I wrote imitations of Beckett's early, incomprehensible English poems, themselves imitations of Eliot. I grew my hair to a length of my choosing. I entered 'Junior College' in Elphinstone College and pretended I was a BA student. I gave off the vibes of a drug addict, without having touched an illegal substance. I made progress on the guitar very fast, and started writing songs when I was sixteen. From a pop-rock singer, I transformed that year to a Canadian singer-songwriter in the making.

The points of entry came then. They formed a small cluster. Maybe it's in their nature to seem like a constellation in retrospect, when one is related to the other. The first was my music teacher's arrival in my life. He wasn't my music teacher then; he was my mother's. He was very young – I realise that now – maybe thirty-four. He wore a white kurta and white pyjamas. His name was Govind Prasad Jaipurwale. My mother had a long list of music teachers in Bombay. However talented they may have been, they were a part of my mother's world, not mine. I mean I wasn't interested in them except as characters in her world, which served as an exotic counterpoint to mine. Govindji, as we called him, was the first of her teachers to access my world. At sixteen, I was ready.

I first heard about him in a conversation a lyricist called Rajesh Johri had with my mother on the balcony of the flat in Malabar Hill. My mother felt her teacher at the time had nothing more to offer her. She and her teachers tired of each other periodically. Rajesh Johri then let drop that surname, Jaipurwale – literally, 'of Jaipur'. It was already known (to my mother, not to me) from his father Laxman Prasad Jaipurwale's reputation as a teacher. 'How good is he?' asked my mother, about the son. Laxman Prasad had, by then, passed on. 'Is he better than X?' she said, referring to her present teacher, a perfectly good singer with, not unusually, alcohol-related problems. 'Better?' said Rajesh Johri. 'X hasn't been born in comparison. *Woh uske samne paida bhi nahin hua.*'

I remember my mother was amused by this recommendation. She repeated it to my father in Rajesh Johri's voice. She was an excellent mimic. And Govindji became her teacher. I was struck by how beautiful his voice was: that, unlike many teachers of classical music whose voice wasn't necessarily their strong point, he could sing the so-called 'light' forms like the bhajans or devotionals my mother wanted to learn from him with quiet, blissful conviction. Just as pure classical music was met with bewilderment, and sometimes mocked, by those who listened to the simpler forms, the simpler forms were slightly looked down upon by the classical world. I use the past tense because classical music is now so peripheral to the consciousness that what I've described no longer constitutes a debate or misunderstanding. Nevertheless, I got the sense that Govindji was walking a tightrope in singing so many forms with such ease; that ease was suspect, and that too much melodiousness risked not being given proper seriousness.

He was a great pleasure to listen to – the tone of his voice, and a mastery that made you believe that he could do anything with it he chose to.

He sang softly, without insistence, and almost never sang the same phrase twice. His aim, achieved with modesty, was to surprise and be surprised.

I wanted to do what he was doing. This was odd, as I'd been content till then to sing songs with my guitar. But there was something contagious, arresting, and disruptive of the flow of time about being able to produce, consecutively, two or three versions of a phrase, each with a marginally different emotional impact, each new thought revising the previous one.

I tried to do it when I was alone, and stumbled. Clearly, you couldn't produce these modulations just because you wanted to.

Not long ago, I found myself discussing narrative with a group of academics over dinner. Someone said that narrative doesn't have to have a beginning, middle, and end in that order. I pointed out that there were narratives in which the beginning took up so much time that you didn't know when you were going to arrive at the actual story. Personally, *that* was the sort of narrative I liked. I told the academics what the filmmaker Gurvinder Singh had said in a talk in Delhi about the screening of his first film *Anhe Ghore da Daan* ('Alms for a Blind Horse') at a film festival in Canada. Singh said that the ten-to-fifteen-minute prologue – which he showed us before his talk – had presented the director of the film festival with a problem. She wanted him to cut it and move straight to the main narrative. He said he'd rather not show the film at all than dispense with the opening. The film's prologue was significant. Nothing happened in it except the establishment of a certain meandering lifelikeness. Since this lifelikeness, this quality of constantly revisiting the present moment, is more important to me than the story, I actually wanted Gurvinder's entire film to have been a prologue.

*

While writing these pages, I wondered if I could call the first chapter 'alaap', thereby playing on the meaning of the main segment of khayal. 'Alaap' means – presumably in all North Indian languages – 'introduction'. It's also a major component of khayal. The initial delineation of the raga, before the vilambit or slow composition starts to the tabla's accompaniment, is called 'alaap'. So is the broaching and exploration of the raga in the vilambit composition, where the singer ascends reluctantly from the lower to the upper tonic, subjecting the notes and the identifying phrases to repeated reinterpretation. This is the alaap too; through a progression of glissandos, it contributes to a full emotional and intellectual engagement with a raga, and can take up to half an hour or more, depending on the singer's inventiveness or obduracy. The alaap is all; its detail justifies the genre's name – 'khayal', Arabic for 'imagination'. From alaap we move to drut, fast-tempo segments, which are more virtuosic, less lyrical and tardy in character. No other music tradition allows the prologue to be definitive in this way; not even the Carnatic or South Indian tradition, or the dhrupad, precursor to the khayal, has a counterpart to the alaap's divagation. Carnatic performance has alapana, a long opening without percussion in which the raga is established. But alapana, like the nom tom alaap in dhrupad, soon takes on a quasi-rhythmic form: that is, the syllables are sung in and out of metre, although percussive accompaniment is still to come in. The rhythmic element in alapana and in the dhrupad's long introductory passages creates a sort of excitement to do with the climactic; in the khayal, though, all expectation of the climactic is set aside. In fact, the rhythmless alaap in khayal is relatively short; the percussion instrument, the tabla, soon joins the singer, playing a tala (a cyclical measure with a fixed number and allocation of beats) at an incredibly retarded tempo. The singer proceeds in free time, heedless of the tala and the tabla player except when they must return, after an interval, with the composition to the one, the first beat, of the time cycle: the sama. Otherwise, unlike Carnatic music or the dhrupad, free time reigns over the exposition, notwithstanding the tabla, which, in a feat of dual awareness, the singer nods to and largely ignores. The alaap is a formal and conceptual innovation of the same family as the circadian novel, in which everything happens, in an amplification of time, before anything's begun to happen. At what point North Indian classical singing allowed itself the liberty of making the introduction – that is, the circumventory exploration that defers, then replaces, the 'main story' – become its definitive movement, I don't know; it could go back to the early twentieth century, when Ustad Abdul Wahid Khan's romantic-modernist proclivities left a deep impress on North Indian performance.

The alaap corresponds with my need for narrative not to be a story, but a series of opening paragraphs, where life hasn't already 'happened', ready for recounting, but is *about* to happen, or is happening, and, as a result, can't be domesticated into a perfect retelling.

Should I call this chapter 'alaap', then? Or should I give the book that name?

If the meeting with Govind Prasad Jaipurwale was a 'point of entry' that drew me to a tradition I'd been indifferent to, there would have been other points of entry before or after which would make me turn to him as a teacher.

I'm speaking of seventies Bombay; a beautiful flat on Malabar Hill; a lifestyle of privilege in a socialist economy, in which 80 per cent of my father's salary was paid in tax; a Bombay in which there was a pretty clear demarcation between the black money that circulated in the business world and the white money my father earned; a Bombay thirteen or fourteen years before deregulation. So – in spite of the privileges that derived from his company position – my father's life remained essentially middle-class. On the one side of us were the untaxed incomes and monetarist-religious values of the business clans; on the other were the deprived, and the educated people who aspired to the sort of life my father had.

My parents had no vanity. This wasn't a conclusion I came to myself, as I'd never subjected them to scrutiny; it was pointed out to me later, when they were old, or gone. The people who said this were right. I don't mean my parents were 'good'. I mean they managed to remain human. For this reason, they spoke to each other in the

Sylheti dialect to the end of their lives. For this reason, we visited relatives annually in towns in North Eastern India like Silchar and Shillong; a liberating experience for all three of us. For this reason, there were hardbound copies of classic Bengali novels on the bookshelves, beside Grolier Classics, the Pelican edition of T. S. Eliot's *Selected Poems*, and biographies of Jackie Onassis and Marilyn Monroe. For this reason, there was music in the house. I mean I had access to much more than a boy in comparable circumstances in Bombay would have had. I don't mean 'culture', or what Bombay deemed to be 'culture'; I mean other worlds.

By 'other worlds', I'm thinking, mainly, of India's modern traditions, which I became aware of through my relatives and through the hardbound volumes on the shelf; and I'm thinking of the classical ones: dance, music, sculpture, temples, mosques. Growing up in Bombay, my friends and I didn't delve into these. We were in our own world, of Sad Sack and Archie, of Elvis and later Dylan. I don't mean we were deracinated; we were a transmutation of Indian reality. We felt Indian, but somehow also felt Woodstock was our inheritance. Something about our formation made us feel naturally at home in the American sixties, a decade that had just passed and gone by, for us, without Vietnam. The English language dominated. In Bombay, the modern Indian languages were called 'vernaculars', and those who spoke them labelled 'vernacs'. I never picked up Marathi, though I was taught it in school. Indian music and Indian traditions felt quasi-religious and therefore discomfiting; we – a secular class that had largely been educated in Christian schools and had no religion ourselves – firmly shut them out.

Still, those 'other worlds' were there, to be skimmed over in textbooks, or, for me, encountered in songs overheard and towns visited.

Some points of entry came to me from lighting on Marathi programmes on TV. I think TV came to Indian households in around 1970, comprising, at first, a few hours every evening about agriculture and industry. Or that's how I remember it. By the mid-seventies, there was a fully functional national channel, which made accommodations for local programming at certain times of day. Then a second channel was added – in Bombay's case, with chiefly Marathi content. Why I chose, in 1978, in that four-bedroom flat in Cuffe Parade, to look beyond the modest English-language entertainment – game shows like *What's the Good Word?* and sitcoms of the *Mind Your Language* variety – towards the Marathi fare, I don't know. But I recall watching some episodes of *Pratibha ani Pratima* (literally, 'Talent and Profile') on Sunday mornings. I saw Kishori Amonkar on this programme, replying to a question and then singing a few notes without any accompaniment. I was struck by the dark flow of the meends or glissandos and the voice's purity. Having ignored Marathi all my life, I understood very little of what was passing between the singer and her interlocutor. It was like watching an arthouse film without subtitles. On another Sunday, I caught Bhimsen Joshi on the same show. At some point, he began to explore, in passionate detail, the notes of a thumri. Once more I felt the urge – as I had with Govindji – to replicate what I'd heard. Once more, I found it near impossible to reproduce what had sounded fluent and spontaneous.

Each encounter – Kishori Amonkar; Bhimsen Joshi; the singer Balgandharva, whom I heard one night on Channel 2 – was a jolt. I think it's safe to say that Balgandharva is almost entirely unknown outside Maharashtra. He was a star in the thirties and forties in a form that's specifically Marathi – 'sangeet natak' or 'music theatre', in which he sang 'natya sangeet': 'theatre music'. He played women. The channel showed pictures of him in a sari. I don't know if I happened upon this programme because, bored by life in Cuffe Parade, I was at a loose end, or because I was scavenging for snippets of classical music, probably being, by now, addicted. The voice was transfixing. It was so high-pitched it could have been a woman's, just as Kesarbai Kerkar's was so low-pitched it could have been a man's. Something spiritual happens when a voice departs its accepted register, which is often determined by gender. This was true of Balgandharva. His singing had a bodiless freedom and pliability. The songs he sang from the natya sangeet repertoire were Marathi offshoots of classical compositions, executed with an almost guileless virtuosity, with Balgandharva clearing his throat before he plunged into a new taan. I had no idea who he was. The programme was Marathi; besides, the channel behaved as if it was radio. The song's name appeared on a wavering caption, and was played from a 78 rpm record.

I should distinguish these equivalents of sightings from J. M. Coetzee's account of overhearing Bach's *Well-Tempered Clavier* in a neighbour's house in suburban Cape Town: 'As long as the music lasted, I was frozen, I dared not breathe.' Intending to overturn a set of questions raised by T. S. Eliot in his 1944 lecture 'What Is a Classic?', Coetzee, in an essay with the same title, asks, 'What does it mean in living terms to say that a classic is what survives? How does such a concept of the classic manifest itself in people's lives?' Answering the question takes Coetzee back to when he was fifteen, and to that experience of Bach. He recounts his rapture, which he had taken as a confirmation of the fact that the classic will eventually speak to you when you're ready to hear it. In retrospect, he interrogates the rapture: a little tortuously, he wonders whether a seemingly transcendental piece of music was 'speaking to me across the ages', as he'd first assumed, or if he was 'symbolically electing high European culture, and command of the codes of that culture, as a route that would take me out of my class position in white South African society . . . of what I must have felt [was] . . . an historical dead end?'

I too had reached a dead end in the twenty-fifth-storey apartment; but it was of another sort. I was alienated not

ALAAP

by marginality but by privilege and its set of duties and rituals. North Indian classical music was not too good for me and my kind. I mean that, despite its pan-Indian status, it didn't have full legitimacy as far as the middle class was concerned. That it was a repository of tradition and authenticity didn't recommend it to teenagers of my generation: if anything, it encouraged us to disengage from it. My parents' generation kept it at arm's length – at least, the educated classes in Bengal seemed to. This might be because classical music was deemed to have some religious content, and educated Bengalis, products of Brahmo reformism, were uneasy with religious content. They preferred the Tagore song, in which devotional material had been disguised, or made invisible. There was spiritual yearning in the Tagore song, but no Radha or Krishna. This absence was crucial to the educated Bengali's spiritual and emotional well-being. Besides, the classical composition belonged to a domain that was neither properly secular nor socialised: its performance was dominated by Muslim ustads and, in the first half of the twentieth century, by tawaifs and baijis – great singers who were also courtesans. This history probably contributed to a maternal uncle's bewilderment when he heard I wanted to learn classical music; it's why my father-in-law, once he began to get to know me, puzzled over my investment in this tradition. The 'classic' occupies a strange place in any culture, hovering between authority and illegitimacy, receiving both reverence and indifference: in India, the reasons for its questionable status have a complex history.

Indian classical music, in other words, couldn't be for me what Bach would have been for Coetzee (though he refuses to give the class analysis the last word). Its impact on me was not a legitimising but a revolutionary one. It isolated me, rather than allowing me to join a club of cognoscenti I might have secretly wanted to be in. This doesn't mean my rapture was timeless; it was, in its way, as timely and historical as Coetzee's, though with other consequences. My discovery of the distinctive Maharashtrian interpretation of classical music was a personal revelation too. As I've said already, I was living in Bombay, the capital of Maharashtra, with – characteristically of my friends and my class – no interest in Marathi culture. To listen to Bhimsen Joshi, for instance, was to understand both the region I'd grown up in and the time – the late seventies – differently. I realised in a few years, when this period of discovery came to an end, partly because I was moving locations, partly because the singers aged, that I'd had access to extraordinary artists: that remarkable creative periods don't necessarily belong to the remote past.

Coetzee recounts that he was 'mooning about' in the back garden when, fifteen years old, he heard *Well-Tempered Clavier*, 'boredom being the main problem of existence in those days'. Boredom was my problem too – although the word encompassed a depthless misery. But my misery was preparing me to notice the world for the first time. I was between sixteen and seventeen that year. I began hiding from friends after my first year in Junior College. One of the reasons was that I didn't want them to know where I lived. I once didn't let in two acquaintances from college – a young man and woman – who'd come to see me: standing at the door in subterfuge, as if there was a dead body inside. The young man said (I wasn't sure if it was an accusation): 'You *live* here?'

Two apartments had been joined to create the flat. This explained its shape: two wings outspread on each side of the doorway. My parents' bedroom was at one end, adjoining a balcony. My small room was next to theirs, with its own balcony, and, on a shelf behind the bed, my personal turntable. Opposite was what was called the 'music room', which had a sofa and a TV, but no other furniture. The floor was covered in coir, and had a rug, so you could sit on the ground, as musicians do in India.

Then, before reaching the front door, was the guest room on the left. Opposite the main doors was a hallway, and the kitchen. The drawing room came next. It had a long balcony looking out on the sea and the Marine Drive. On the right was the dining room. The drawing room had a record player, around which we occasionally congregated. At the very end was my father's study, which he hardly went to – maybe because, once he was home, he spent all his time with my mother.

In my parents' record collection, which I'd been foraging into, I found some Western classical music, acquired as a duty when they were in London: a box set of Beethoven's symphonies, conducted by Herbert von Karajan, the dirty vinyl surfaces protected by white sleeves. It – like a record of the West End version of *My Fair Lady* – was part of the cargo that had come back in 1961 from England. Despite knowing little about Western classical music (and slightly prejudiced against it), I began to listen to Beethoven.

I'd never given Western classical music a proper chance, not because I disliked it, but because I disliked its followers: I'd noticed that most Indians who enthused over it were tone-deaf. They had clearly acquainted themselves with it for reasons other than pleasure. They mentioned the names of compositions as if referring to privileged friends. There were exceptions – the filmmaker Satyajit Ray, whose contribution to musical scores for cinema was profound; and the Parsis of Bombay, who had produced Zubin Mehta (and, in another genre, Freddie Mercury).

I quickly became familiar with four of the symphonies – the Fifth, of course; the Sixth, the 'Pastoral'; the Seventh, my favourite; and the Ninth.

While listening to the second movement of the Seventh, gripped by its charged progress, I found myself looking, beyond the penthouse opposite that was being made for the builder's daughter, at the sky. Unlike other parts of Bombay and India, there was a deadness to earth and water in Cuffe Parade, because it was land that had been recently reclaimed for development. And I was on the twenty-fifth floor, in a state of elevation that's unnatural to an Indian. I was cut off from the world. The context was an appropriate one for listening to Western classical music, which, to my ears, had a closedness about it – the finality of an artefact. Looking out at the sky and the massive clouds, I could construct majestic inner narratives while listening to the Seventh; and the Fifth. I became prone to receiving Beethoven in this dramatic narrative way. There's something about Western music that lends itself, for the lay listener and for anyone attuned to the culture that produced it, to representation. There are many like Helen in *Howards End*, who, on hearing the Fifth Symphony, 'sees heroes and shipwrecks in the music's flood'. Or the listener's passion could be mirrored, in the music, by Beethoven's life: 'He brought back the gusts of splendour, the hero-ism, the youth, the magnificence of life and death, and, amidst vast roarings of a superhuman joy, he led the Fifth Symphony to its conclusion.' Helen's imaginings, and my own inchoate storytelling while I listened to the Fifth in my small room, have a history. The Fifth became known early on as 'Schicksals-Sinfonie', or 'symphony of destiny'. Beethoven was going deaf while compos-ing it; so the biographical narrative of impediment and triumph are inextricable from the music's effect on the lay, but acculturated, listener. The first enraptured critical response, by E. T. A. Hoffmann in 1810 in the *Allgemeine musikalische Zeitung*, is heavily narratolog-ical: 'Radiant beams shoot through this region's deep night, and we become aware of gigantic shadows which, rocking back and forth, close in on us . . .' Studying clouds from the twenty-fifth storey, I constructed – without necessarily meaning to – comparable epics around von Karajan's Beethoven.

The Sixth, which engrossed me less than the works I've mentioned, but which I found pleasing, lent itself especially to my storytelling urges. I didn't feel these urges were wrong; without knowing why, I assumed they were a valid response to music. While listening to the 'Pastoral', I was stirred by images of meadows, trees, weather, and valleys I'd never known – just as a period film is incomplete without an appropriate score, a score requires the right kind of visual accompaniment: not an actual film, but one you're making up in your head. It's possible, listening to the Sixth, to invent a landscape you've never known as if it had been bequeathed to you, in the way we're told that the brain can fabricate memories. Being Indian, I certainly hadn't encountered the world I now spontaneously generated while listening, except in picture books, paintings, and movies. Surely *none* of us has. Yet listening to the 'Pastoral' gave to that world a wholeness and continuity it can't possibly have now, if it ever did.

Of course, the Sixth has programmatic content; Beethoven had tied it to a narrative, and, as a result, to emotional and historical verisimilitude. By 'verisimilitude', I don't just mean an approximation of reality, but a confirmation of what we already know, through conventions, to be real. The first movement has to do with the arrival in the countryside; the second with walking by a brook; the third with country folk gathered to dance; the fourth with a thunderstorm; the fifth with a shepherd's song in the post-storm lull. As we produce our home movie in our heads, the fact that much of the symphony is in a major key feels right too: F major, and B flat major for the second movement. How could such uplifting episodes to do with natural beauty and sunlight be translated into anything but the major mode? The major scale, in post-Enlightenment Western culture, is the musical counterpart to, and expression of, happiness. Since the Aristotelian schema, which defines much of Western culture, gives a minor aesthetic value to the comic or joyous, it follows that the major should be minor, or less serious; major works in the major mode *should* be the exception rather than the norm. There are any number of great compositions in the major scales in the classical period, but, with Beethoven, the extreme individuality of his romantic phase is contained, for the lay contemporary listener whose tastes have been shaped by romanticism, in the minor keys of the Fifth and Ninth, and the Seventh's arresting second movement. Midway through the ebullient interlude in the Seventh's first movement in A major, when we hear three chromatic notes descending emphatically – F#, F (the flat sixth), and E – our mood, fleetingly, becomes grave: an intimation of the minor has been introduced to the major. The major scale to us is the scale of happiness, a minor emotion; the minor or dissonant scales are the scales of deeper and major shifts in emotional register. It's right, then, that the fourth movement of the 'Pastoral' – the storm – should migrate to F minor. For the lay listener, the major and minor keys in European music are inseparable from mimesis.

Some works in the European musical tradition have overt representational content; they're *about* something, and they mimic what they're about. *Flight of the Bumblebee* comes to mind; *Peter and the Wolf*; *Pictures at an Exhibition*. But it seems that the reception of *all* Western music is predominantly located for the ordinary listener in a mimetic ethos, pertaining not just to particular compositions, but to the happy and sad scales, and, on the opposite pole, the difficult twentieth-century developments of dissonance and atonality, which are occasionally presumed to represent in some way the trauma of the modern (that is, the European modern): the breakdown of cultures, civilisations, and selves.

This mimetic quality makes Western music the natural choice for scoring movies. The deep link between sound and narrative imagery in Western culture is exemplified by the fact that there's hardly any cinema without background music. To not hear a tune set to a major key when the day is sunny and the windows open, or when the protagonist has received a long-awaited appointment letter or fallen in love, is unimaginable. To not have notes in a minor key accompany loss, separation, or farewell is similarly rare. Suspense and terror are augmented by dissonance, or chromatic notes in dizzying succession. Thinking mimetically is encouraged: subtitles on Prime Video don't say 'loud' or 'soft' music, or 'slow' or 'fast', but 'tense music' or 'cheerful music'.

Instruments participate in mimesis: flutes, oboes, and bassoon reproduce bird calls in the 'Pastoral', and avian excitement in *Peter and the Wolf*; in the latter, the harrumphing bassoon embodies the grandfather. These effects are noted with delight by the audience because, presumably, tonality had been anthropomorphised by the late eighteenth century. This means that classical music could later be used with comic timing in visual narratives that emerged alongside cinema, like the Disney cartoon or Hanna-Barbera's *Tom and Jerry*, which themselves comprise wonderful anthropomorphic dramas.

Tempo, too, signals the protagonist's journey: psychological, spiritual, physical. Adagio isn't just a slow movement; it has connotations of emotional heaviness. The slowness of alaap in khayal, by contrast, is unrelated to human allegory. Expansiveness of form gives centre-stage to the raga rather than the human.

I use the word 'narrative' not just to describe the connection between a piece of European classical music and a specific programme, as in *Peter and the Wolf*. I mean the tradition's location, for many of us, in the narrative of the human. What Brecht says about European proscenium theatre is pertinent to music: 'Its story is arranged in such a way as to create "universal" situations that allow man with a capital M to express himself: man of every period and every colour. All its incidents are just one enormous cue, and this cue is followed by the "external" response: the inevitable, usual, natural, purely human response.'

Indian films *can* be scored with Indian classical music on narrative principles, because mimesis is malleable to new purposes and contexts. To give only one instance, raga Todi, whose second, third, and sixth notes are flat, has been used as background in Hindi films in scenes of mourning. But this has little to do with the way it's sung, or played by instrumentalists. Todi is a morning raga; like other ragas, it resists interpretation, and is undertaken by musicians both as a formal exploration and a meditation. The flat notes have formal and meditative implications, not humanistic ones, whereby they'd represent sadness. I say this firmly, as a singer and listener, despite Bharata's well-known theory, in the second century, of rasa (literally, 'juice', or an emotion that can be 'tasted' via performance). For Bharata, music and dance have eight rasas: sringara, to do with the erotics of adornment; hasyam, or laughter; karuna, pity; raudram, anger; bibhatsam, or the grotesque; bhayanaka, terror; veer, heroic; and adbhut, wonder. But the way music and the arts developed in India, moving towards the formal, the meditative, meant that the ninth, most significant rasa needed to be added a few centuries later – a non-narrative one: shant, or tranquil.

Scoring films with Indian classical music can also be based on pure misunderstanding, as in Pasolini's version of *Medea*. Pasolini uses a few notes from the dhrupad singers, the Dagar brothers, to suggest foreboding, possibly because the music and singing style sound alien to him. In the dhrupad itself, those notes would comprise a dwelling on the raga – they'd have no added meaning. Their proper visual accompaniment would be a blank screen.

Satyajit Ray, maybe the most musically intelligent of the arthouse auteurs, and unusual in being an Indian who was beholden to Western classical music, recognised mimesis, and the lack of it, in music as a problem of a particular order for the filmmaker. According to Ray, who began scoring his films early on, there was an 'absence of a dramatic narrative tradition in Indian music':

> It is valid to speak of a Beethoven symphony in terms of universal brotherhood, or man's struggle against fate or the passionate outpourings of a soul in torment. Western classical music underwent a process of humanisation with

the invention of the sonata form – with its masculine first subjects and feminine subjects and their interweaving and progress through a series of dramatic key-changes, to a point of culmination . . . But a *raga* is a *raga*.

*

I was listening to von Karajan's Beethoven in that apartment, building castles in the air as I did so, but I was also starting to grapple with Indian classical music. Well before I'd made sense of the talas, or knew how to fill up the temporal space of the khayal, I realised that the raga's relationship to the world was different from Western music's. Standing between conflicting points of reference, I had to navigate my way.

It's not possible to do any more than hint at what the difference is. One way of describing it might be that, as children, worldwide, of the European Enlightenment, we assume that the relationship between a human-engendered form and reality has to do with representation: that story, art, and music must in some way represent the world. If they choose not to, it's an act of rebellion, or of transcendence. But how do we understand an aesthetic whose response to the world arises from homage rather than the matter of representational fidelity to an inner or outer life?

Indian artists who have experienced both the Western musical tradition and the Indian, and have worked in domains that might opt to be representational or abstain from representation – like literature or cinema – have been sensitive to the cultural particularities of this question. I've referred to Ray above, and the way he uses, in a 1965 essay, the phrase 'dramatic narrative tradition' as a euphemism for a post-Renaissance lineage. 'A raga is a raga' is reminiscent of 'A rose is a rose is a rose', Gertrude Stein's pithy assertion of modernism's non-representational turn.

In 1894, Tagore was thinking of similar things while overseeing, as a young man, his father's estates as he journeyed up the river Shilaidaha in a house boat. 'Last night, not very late,' he writes in a letter to his niece, 'I was woken by the sound of water. A great tumult and powerful restlessness had suddenly come to the river.' The nocturnal stillness and the unexpected sound prompt categorisations to do with music. Tagore is both troubled and liberated by the fact that he can't take it as a given; that he can't accept, as people of his generation would have been asked to, that harmony is a *development* on melody; that melody is simply a more primordial musical form. For him, these terms are situated in world views that respond, among other things, differently to the human and the representational.

> If you wake up and sit like this in the middle of the night, in the midst of such a scene, you feel as if you and the

world are somehow in some way made anew, as if the
world of daylight and commerce with men had become
utterly untrue. Again, waking up this morning, how far
away and indistinct that world of my night seems to have
become. For man, both are true, yet both are terribly
independent of one another. It seems to me as if the world
of the day is European music – in tune and out of tune,
in part and in the whole – coming together like a huge
forceful tangle of *harmony*, and the world of the night
is our Indian music, a pure, tender, serious, unmixed
rāginī. Both move us, yet both are opposed to each other.
There's a hesitation and a tremendous opposition right at
the root of nature, where everything is divided between
king and queen – there's nothing we can do about it: day
and night, variety and wholeness, the expressive and the
timeless. We Indians live in that kingdom of night. We
are entranced by that which is timeless and whole. Ours
is the song of personal solitude, Europe's is that of social
accompaniment. Our music takes the listener outside of
the limits of man's everyday vicissitudes to that lonely
land of renunciation that is at the root of the entire
universe, while Europe's music dances variously to the
endless rise and fall of man's joys and sorrows.

(trans. Rosinka Chaudhuri)

'We Indians live in that kingdom of night': it's the
non-representational tendency of the raga that Tagore
is referring to – its abjuring of portrayal. Tagore's words

make me think of the singer Kishori Amonkar saying to an interviewer in 1991, in the context of Indian classical music, that, in a music that explores notes alone, outside the framework of song or rhythm, you sing blind, as it were. You can neither see nor touch notes, she reminds her interlocutor.

Tagore's deliberate use of the English word 'harmony' sets up a parallel between Western music and the realist novel. The 'world of the day', 'social accompaniment', and 'the endless rise and fall of man's joys and sorrows' – these phrases echo D. H. Lawrence's claim that the novel is the 'highest complex of subtle interrelatedness that man has discovered'. For the ragini, Tagore sets up an implicit comparison with poetry: non-narrative; non-representational; 'the world of night'. The subjectivity of these siftings don't make them less important or immediate.

Mani Kaul, the most strikingly non-narrative of the Indian arthouse filmmakers of the sixties and seventies, was also a student and exponent of the dhrupad. I don't know if it was his exposure to the raga that made his films (according to many) notoriously slow, and Kaul (this is known to relatively few) a ferocious critic of the Renaissance. The Renaissance painting, like proscenium theatre, or, indeed, the realist story, gives centre-stage to a protagonist – that is, the human being. Renaissance art's development of perspective helps consolidate the rules of realism: a foreground or central theme, and a background occupied by what's necessary to complete the portrait of the protagonist. Kaul's cinema wished to be unfettered by hero or theme; he wanted the camera to devote itself equally to recording things ordinarily consigned to 'background'.

Giving a talk, Kaul reminded his audience how 'foreground' and 'background' have also, since the Renaissance, informed Western musical performance and composition. This is true to an extent: in harmony, the background might be indispensable, but, to many, it's of secondary status. We listen first to what's in the foreground – like the frenetic violins in *Flight of the Bumblebee*, noting in passing the cellos that create the backdrop. We visualise the bee's path in a three-dimensional setting. This sense of spatial depth directs how we listen even when the composition isn't overtly shaped by a narrative. In dhrupad or khayal, the tanpura isn't background; it's a weave.

There's no one thing called 'the Renaissance' any more than there's a 'Western music', or even a 'Western thought' (as in Derrida's sweeping enquiry into the 'history of metaphysics in Western thought'). Yet the critiques I've mentioned have compulsions: compulsions experienced by artists who, as they work between traditions, become aware of the fragility of the seemingly immemorial ways in which we think of those traditions.

*

Every raga in North Indian music has a time, and sometimes a season, of performance: it can't, or shouldn't, be performed in contravention of the time of day or season it's linked to – it would be plain odd if it were. Kedar is sung after eight o'clock in the evening, and to sing it at twilight, at 6 p.m., would create slight discomfiture. I needn't mention the incredulity a singer would face if they performed Kedar in the morning.

The same holds true of a seasonal raga like Megh (literally, 'cloud'), which is added to the repertoire specifically for the duration of the monsoons. It would be strange to hear a musician playing Megh in January.

Of course, Western music has time-adhering chants, and evensong; but their origins go back to pre-Renaissance religious practice or to liturgy. Their location is church or monastery, and these provenances don't impact on what we now understand as a concert performance. The raga has long ceased to be temple-specific, if it ever was: it's a way of experiencing the world. Its connection to time and season should also be distinguished from the tonally beautiful, hour-of-the-day-related call of the muezzin.

Ragas are discussed in Bharata's treatise on performance, *Natya Shastra* (second century BCE). But there's no mention of the constraints of time and season in the *Natya Shastra*; according to the scholar Mukund Lath, seasonal proprieties for ragas surface in texts from the tenth and eleventh centuries; the proprieties of time in the twelfth. So the very particular, and peculiar, relationship between the raga and the world has been with us for roughly seven or eight hundred years.

There is no obvious, or mimetic, or representational, or narrative, connection between a raga and a time of day or season, as there is, say, between Beethoven's Sixth Symphony and spring, nature, and the countryside. An evening raga might be predominantly in the major mode, like Kedar and Chhaya Nat; it could have flats in the second and sixth notes, and a sharp fourth, like Puriya Dhanashree or Paraj; it could have a flat third, sixth, and seventh, like Darbari. However, the morning ragas Asavari and Jaunpuri also have the same flat third, sixth, and seventh. The springtime raga, Basant, has the same flats and sharps as the evening raga, Purvi; so does the morning raga, Lalita Gauri. The morning raga Bilawal, which is a major scale, has almost the same notes as the evening ragas Kedar, Khamaj, and Desh, the monsoon raga Gaud Malhar, and the afternoon raga Gaud Sarang.

What I mean is that there are no scales or sets of notes in North Indian classical music that have a reliable mimetic identity, by which we can safely associate them with morning or night, light or dark, joy or sadness. The relationship that the raga has to time or day or season – that is, to the world – is not narrative or representational, but linguistic; I mean the

39

relationship between raga Kedar and evening is as arbitrary and ineluctable as the relationship between the word 'evening' itself and that time of day. Arbitrary, in that 'evening', as a term, has no inherent evening-like qualities; unlike onomatopoeic words – say, 'glug' – its sound doesn't mimic what it means. Yet the relationship is ineluctable too. Once we're aware of language – and who isn't? – it *becomes*, for us, the world it refers to. To use 'morning' to refer to 'evening' would lead to dissonance. Similarly, to sing the morning raga Bhairav in the evening is not so much inadmissible as incongruous. Once we're aware of the ragas, they become part of what can only be called a linguistic or textual consciousness of the world in the present moment, the world being, in this case, 'India' or 'North India'. Music becomes a text which is not so much *about* the world, but which is, like language, our way of both being in and deciphering it, its waning and returning of light, its subtle changes of weather. Given the representational quality of the 'Pastoral' Symphony, given it's 'about' spring, it's perfectly possible to perform it when it's *not* spring; that is, all year round. The 'Pastoral' is a narrative or representation that can be undertaken at any time. Given the linguistic and textual character of Hindustani classical music, Basant, the springtime raga, must be performed only in the spring; the season and weather, and not just the notes of the composition, are part of the raga's textuality. The raga is not *about* the

40

world; it's of it. Once you know the raga, the world and it can't be independent of each other, in the way it's impossible to grasp the physical universe outside of the language in which we think and feel. As the raga is of the world, its primary space isn't a concert space, or even the temples and courts in which it once unfolded; it's situated really in a time of day or season, and – in contrast to how we experience music in a concert hall – a significant leakage in both directions is allowed: the raga's into the world, the world's into the raga. For this reason, every sound – birdcall; a car horn; a cough – is continuous with its textuality and texture. I probably first began to notice the everyday (as a seventeen- or eighteen-year-old) through Indian music's reordering of my idea of what a relationship with my surroundings comprised. As a result of this situatedness, a raga that's sung at a time of day it's not meant for is subjected, in the critic Raghava Menon's words, to 'jet lag'. The metaphor of intercontinental travel emphasises the textuality of North Indian classical music. When I practise the morning raga Todi in Oxford, I feel an incompatibility. This is because the morning in Oxford is not only a different reality; it's a different language. The problem of making Todi fit is a translational one.

I'm not claiming that the raga belongs organically to the Indian landscape. I'm saying that, while language is local and provisional, it's also how we experience the universe. As Hindustani classical music reminds us, 'India' is text. Only a relatively small bit of reality can be conveyed by narrating stories 'about' it, or representing it in pictures. We participate in reality by experiencing language at its most arbitrary, basic level of meaning: Kedar is evening; Bhairav is morning; 'evening' is the time that occurs before night. This constant embrace of language is how we elect to live in the world. The singer is reminded of this every time they sing a raga. One also concedes that a culture that privileges narrative and representation also privileges the author who gives birth to the piece of representation; as with Beethoven. A culture that gives primacy to language, as with the North Indian classical music tradition, will relegate the composer to secondary or invisible status, and see text as the primary progenitor; this is why most ragas have no known composers, and who the composer might be is of secondary interest.

What is a raga? The question can be approached in many ways, and I'll restrict myself for now to the context I've established, of Indian music as text or language. The raga has no more an absolute identity than a word does. Ferdinand de Saussure's claim that language is a social fabric marked by 'difference' is especially true of ragas. There's nothing about the word 'bat', for example, that makes it intrinsically refer to that animal. 'Bat' – as is the case with other words – is not an absolute; it's a sign and a sound that's related to all the similar sounds and signs it is not: like 'bed', or 'bud', or 'but'. This is what Saussure means by 'difference': the way language and its meanings are formed by negative differentiations. Similarly, 'evening' means what it does not because it has an automatic link with that time of day, but because its sound distinguishes itself from other sounds that have different meanings: 'avenue' and 'awning', for instance. Derrida, in recognition of Saussure's insight that the word isn't born with an eternal, fixed identity, poetically calls this lack of fixity, this residue of one sound in another, a 'trace'.

This is one way of looking at the raga. It has no recognisable existence in isolation from other ragas. It is recognisable through differentiation; it is the ragas that it is not. So the default response of the critic or pedant to a performance is to look not for faulty pitch or lack of technique, but to do with an absence of mindfulness on the performer's part concerning how one raga might end up, if they're not careful, becoming another one. 'His Marwa often sounded like Puriya, and at times became Sohini too,' the critic might remark, in relation to three ragas that have identical notes: a flat re or second note, a natural ga or third, a sharp ma or fourth, and a natural dha and ni, or sixth and seventh. Marwa identifies itself by abstaining gracefully from the tonic, and visiting it sparely; by dwelling largely on the relationship between the flat re or second and the natural dha or sixth. Puriya evolves far more linearly; Sohini jumps straight to the upper tonic, and compositions in this raga hover in the high register. Each of these ragas is unmistakable; each is also a trace.

What is a raga?

To answer this question we must first acquire a sense of what it isn't. It isn't a composition, though compositions are set to ragas. It isn't a melody, in that a melody can be sung without preoccupations to do with form and shape; with the raga, the emergence during its exposition of its rupa – the features and shape that make it recognisable for what it is alongside other forms in the world – is of primary importance.

A raga is not a scale. Its notes ascend and descend, but not in the linear manner in which a scale's does. The raga is not the sum total of its notes. You may know the notes of a raga, but have little idea of what it is.

I share these thoughts because of confusions I had to sort out when I began to learn from Govindji. I want to return to them here, alongside my first experiences of unravelling the kind of thinking the raga comprises. Govindji certainly didn't tell me what a raga was. An unconventional singer and man, he, nevertheless, began by giving me the rudiments of the raga according to the conventions of contemporary, post-Bhatkande teaching. Vishnu Narayan Bhatkande (1860–1936) was a modern organiser of thousands of North Indian ragas. He came up with the idea – the scheme – that all ragas derived from one or another of ten parent scales, which he called thaats. The theory already had a seventeenth-century counterpart in Carnatic music; besides, thaats are to be found in that period in Sanskrit and Persian texts as practical aids. As a classificatory tool, the parent-scale theory had a precursor, it seems to me, in the scholar William Jones's work in late-eighteenth-century Calcutta on the Indo-European languages: research that established that several languages in the world are offshoots of certain ancient ones, like Sanskrit, Persian, Greek, and Latin. Bhatkande's classificatory legacy is influential, but at first I found it puzzling. Misleadingly, the names of the ten parent scales, or thaats, are also the names of ragas. But a thaat is not a raga: why not?

Govindji made me write the thaats down.

1 The first one in my notebook was Bilawal:

sa re ga ma pa dha ni sa

That is, akin to the seven notes of the C major scale, with no sharps or flats.

Bilawal must have been the first on my list because, being the major scale, it was the easiest to sing. But singing the major scale, up and down, doesn't at all mean that you're singing raga Bilawal. The latter might share the same notes as the major scale, but is by no means identical with it. Raga Bilawal, like all ragas, is a particular progression of notes. It climbs from the lower to the upper tonic in roughly these phases:

(phase 1, arising from the lower tonic)	sa ga ma re sa
	sa ga ma ga pa
	pa dha dha (touches ni flat) ga
	ga ma pa ma ga
	ga ma re sa
(phase 2, rising to the upper tonic)	ga ma re ga ma ga pa
	pa ni dha ni **sa re sa**
	sa ni dha pa ma ga
	ga ma re sa

Here is Bhatkande's Bilawal thaat:

sa re ga ma pa dha ni sa
sa ni dha pa ma ga re sa

Even if you weren't to hum the notes to yourself, you can spot the difference between the thaat and the raga by looking at their appearance on the page. The thaat looks like a recumbent spine. The raga, even transcribed approximately, has an indeterminate, emergent shape. Notice that the way the thaat is written down – sa re ga ma pa – represents a straightforward onward movement. The raga Bilawal, however, evades a linear ascent, as do

47

all ragas. It skips the second note, goes straight to ga, the third; returns to the second, then climbs up again. If I were to sing sa re ga ma pa (the first five notes of the thaat), I would be singing not Bilawal but Chhaya Nat, in which the notes *may* progress in that manner. The thaat, then, is a confusing Bhatkandean abstraction. The raga's a form whose features don't become clearer – if anything, they become less clear – by knowing what the thaats are.

I point this out because, eager to learn Indian classical music in 1978, I took down the notes of the ten thaats as dictated to me by Govindji, and assumed I then knew ten ragas. The fact that the thaats had the names of ragas made it plausible to assume they *were* ragas. I sang sa re ga ma pa dhi ni sa and thought I was singing Bilawal. Soon, I started to doubt that this was true.

The names of the other nine thaats are:

2 Kalyan

This is identical to the major scale, except that it has a sharp ma or fourth. The raga called 'Kalyan' is hardly ever sung today, at least among performers of Hindustani classical music (Kalyani, with the same notes, is common in concerts of Carnatic music). In North Indian music, it exists only in a hyphenated partnership with other ragas. For instance, raga Yaman has the same notes as the Kalyan thaat; and there's Yaman Kalyan, which occasionally introduces the natural ma or fourth to emotional effect. Then there's raga Shuddha Kalyan (literally, 'pure' Kalyan), which, as it happens, isn't quite pure, resembling raga Bhupali and omitting the fourth altogether in the ascent, incorporating Kalyan's sharp ma in the descent alone. These apparent inconsistencies are a reminder that it takes a nuanced accounting of differences to spot a raga.

Let's have a quick look at Yaman, the raga whose notes are the same as the Kalyan thaat's. I'm going to restrict myself to discussing how it ascends to the fifth note, pa, and not concern myself with its onward climb to the upper tonic, or **sa**, as the first five notes themselves give the interpreter a great deal of material to work with and think about.

As with every raga, the performer will begin at the lower sa, the tonic. This is both a point of entry and a meditative reference-point. *Meditative* reference-point; not a standardising one, as the natural C inadvertently came to be in Western music. C major, because of the predominance of the piano, and because it's played on the piano's white keys without sharps or flats, is the benchmark or default scale against which other keys and scales, sharps and flats are measured. Among its many functions are those to do with implicitly governing and bringing order to the family of notes and scales over which it rules. There's no concept of a default scale, to which other scales and notes habitually refer back, in Indian music.

The role that sa plays in governance is secondary. It's a reference-point for meditation because it's where the raga begins and ends. As sa isn't a beginning alone, but also the end, it's an element that has a unique independence and sovereignty. It's the note that the singer can stay with for as long as they choose, as listeners wait, agog, for the raga to eventually commence. During practice, the sa can be explored outside the raga's interrelationship of notes; the singer can keep repeating and inhabiting it, as if the raga itself had become temporarily irrelevant.

As each raga is nothing but a specific shape and form, one of the characteristics of a raga may include the occasional avoidance of the sa. This is true of Yaman, especially in the ascent (arohan). The singer begins with sa. Yet Yaman's first note isn't sa, but *ni*, the lower seventh. In the sketch below, of a beginning for Yaman, I've put the sa in parentheses whenever it's absent or unmentioned.

sa
ni (sa) re ga re sa
ni (sa) re ga re má ga
má pa
pa re sa

I've put sa in brackets because it's often elided in observance of Yaman's form. Like other ragas, Yaman deals as much with evasion as it does with expression. In fact, evasion, in an exposition, is a recurrent form of expression. Also, the parenthetical sa reminds us again how unlike the thaat the raga, with its various indecisions, is. See, too, the fourth line above: má, pa. In Western music, we think of the seventh as the note that yearns for resolution or completion, as it strives for the upper tonic. In Indian music, there are *at least* two notes that desire completion or fulfilment: the seventh and, as in Yaman, the sharp fourth, which strains to climb to the fifth's (pa's) calm and solidity. A slow and lingering tension is contained in my shorthand in the fourth line: má, pa.

Glance at the final, fifth line above. Before the raga progresses further, it must descend and reconcile itself with the sa, as if to remind itself of the moment of its beginning. But, with a stoic dignity, it won't go down the familiar linear steps: pa má ga re sa. It *could*; Yaman doesn't prohibit the linear descent; but linearity is clumsy, and grace comes from looking askance – so, the fourth and third notes are to be ignored, in a kind of pretence, and, from the pa, the raga returns to sa via an imperious glissando to the second note: pa re sa. In this way, the features of Yaman as an individual living thing become discernible.

Bhatkande makes the abstraction 'Kalyan' Yaman's parent. But there are longstanding accounts that the raga's origins lie with Amir Khusro, the poet, Sufi mystic, musician, and intellectual in the Delhi sultanate in the thirteenth and fourteenth centuries. Khusro was born

51

in 1253 and died in 1325; he was the son of Turkish migrants. Excited by the inadvertent gift bequeathed to him, of being born in India, he apparently called himself 'Turk-e-hindavi': 'Indian Turk' or 'Hindu Turk'. Khusro, like other great artists in the country after him, is constantly alert to the creative possibilities being in India offers; he seems, in that sense, to be the first self-conscious Indian. Perhaps it requires not nationalism but a degree of estrangement and unfamiliarity to understand and celebrate what being Indian is; as was the case in the early nineteenth century with Henry Louis Vivian Derozio, a young Anglo-Portuguese poet who died at the age of twenty-two, but not before he'd had a significant influence on a generation of students in Calcutta, and declared himself an 'Indian', and elegised the ruins of his 'glorious' country in English sonnets that are studied by schoolchildren today. Khusro is remarkable because he may also be the world's first Renaissance man, experimenting with genre a few hundred years before the European Renaissance. For now, I wish to note my memory of reading, in a biography of Khusro, of how he was struck by a tune a Yemeni merchant visiting Delhi was humming to himself. The tune appealed to Khusro; he memorised it, calling it 'Yaman', after the country the merchant came from. There's more than one account of how Khusro conceived the raga; I like this one for its plausibility to do with how a creative work is engendered, almost always at a crossroads. Besides being composers or writers, many of the artists who determine the direction traditions take are, like Khusro, collectors. Tagore was another; he collected tunes, then transformed them. I recall my wife drawing my attention to passages in *Jibaner Jhara Pata* ('Life's Fallen Leaves'), a memoir by Tagore's niece Sarala Debi Chaudhurani, in which she describes the state of receptivity and excitement in which the Tagore family gathered tunes from passers-by and itinerants and hawkers, melodies later turned by Tagore into songs. Yaman too is very possibly the result of a similar transformation.

3 Purvi
The second and sixth notes in the thaat are flat; the fourth is sharp. In raga Purvi, the natural fourth is introduced intermittently as the first five notes are explored. It creates a departure in the elaboration. Without the occasional natural fourth, Purvi becomes Puriya Dhanashree.

4 Khamaj
According to the thaat, this is identical to the major scale, except for the seventh note, which is flat. The raga, unlike the thaat, has both a natural and a flat seventh. The latter is only sung or played in the descent. This is important, because only in a downward glissando from the upper sa or tonic, touching the natural seventh in passing as it glides down, does the flat seventh or ni carry an aura of loss. Going up, the natural ni has a

sharpness about it; it's trying to attain the sa. Coming down, the flat ni is already in the region of regret. Very quickly, those three notes, which constitute a dipping triangle as the singer arrives at and departs the high **sa** –

             sa

     ni

             ni

– make us conscious that a great deal (time; a world) has passed.

5 Kafi

The third and seventh notes are flat in the thaat. The raga is almost never sung in its pure form, but in its 'mishra' or 'impure' one, in which both the normal and flat third are used to great emotional effect, reminiscent of the impact of the two nishads, or sevenths, in Khamaj.

6 Asavari

The third, sixth, and seventh notes are flat in the thaat, as they are in the raga. In Western music, its equivalent is the generically 'sad' Aeolian mode. The raga can be distinguished by the way it jumps straight from the first and second notes to the fourth, dwells briefly on its curious grandeur (the fourth, in many musical systems, is a fresh beginning), then moves to the fifth, and touches the flat sixth, reflecting – again briefly – on its pathos,

54

reaches resolution with the upper tonic (or **sa**), then at once plangently returns to the flat sixth, arrives at the fifth's temporary resting place, before going back to the tonic where it began, touching the ruminative flat third on the way down. Raga Asavari, then, combines a sense of the inaugural in its leaps to the fourth and fifth; and a backward-lookingness in its recurrent caressing (only in the descent) of the flat third and sixth (ga and dha).

7 Bhairav

sa <u>re</u> ga ma pa <u>dha</u> ni **sa**

The second and sixth notes are flat. The thaat is more or less the same as the raga, which is sung in the morning. Many singers start their day practising Bhairav. I learnt it from my teacher's brother-in-law, Hazarilal, who instructed me that I should remember to pause at ma during the arohan. So:

sa ga <u>re</u> sa

sa ma

ma pa

ga ma <u>dha</u> pa

ga ma <u>re</u> sa

Such simplicity. Although we're only barely midway through a perfunctory sketch of the raga at this point, the notes are amenable – even while keeping the ma in mind – to any number of combinations. It's morning; we're uninvolved in the day's routine. Bhairav is witness to a renewal; a re-entry into the regime of music.

8 Todi

This is a raga I'm more familiar with than any other. At least I should be: I've been singing it almost every morning for decades. It's the raga of my day's first riyaaz, or practice. Yet I'm never bored of it (feeling jaded by practice is another matter), and possibly never sing it in the same way twice. This must mean that, despite the years I've spent with it, I still don't know Todi completely. Each morning, I dwell on/in it for an hour, revisiting the same sequence of vilambit, madhya laya (medium tempo), and drut compositions. Sometimes I'll approach a section or feature in a way I haven't before. This doesn't mean I depart the raga's form; I can't, and, more importantly, don't want to. I mean I'm temporarily possessed by a fresh interpretation or mood.

Unlike Bhatkande's thaat, there is, at present (as far as I know), no raga called just 'Todi'. The raga has a number of variants, but the two major ones are Gujri Todi and Miyan ki Todi, both of which I explore in my morning riyaaz.

The adjective 'Gujri' in 'Gujri Todi' hints at the raga's regional or folk or rural beginnings. The Gujjars are a pastoral clan in Northern and North West India,

Pakistan, and Afghanistan. Todi may have been a tune that the Gujjars sang. Any raga represents an aesthetic and intellectual transformation of folk or other varieties of scales not only into a particular formal progression, but into material for the most minute enquiry, as well as meditation. Gujri Todi has six notes:

sa <u>re</u> <u>ga</u> má <u>dha</u> ni

It's a complex melody, in that it has three flat notes and a sharp fourth. The sharp fourth, má, doesn't, however, lead to a resolution in the fifth, the pancham or pa, as is the case usually, because there *is* no fifth in Gujri Todi. So, if you set aside the tonic, you can sing it as a five-note or pentatonic scale, such as the blues scale is: <u>re</u> <u>ga</u> má <u>dha</u> ni. As you lose yourself in the five notes, the inevitable return to sa is almost like a sudden awakening.

Bhatkande, of course, dispenses with all this. His Todi thaat is a linear scale with the fifth intact:

sa <u>re</u> <u>ga</u> má pa <u>dha</u> ni

Now, there's a variant called Miyan ki Todi which does incorporate the fifth, but in a way that the Todi thaat is incapable of capturing.

What is Miyan ki Todi? Literally, the words translate as 'Miyan's Todi'. Who or what is 'Miyan'? (The closing 'n' is silent except as a nasal inflection on the second syllable.) 'Miyan' is a respectful honorific in Urdu, something between 'sir' and 'mister'. Here, it refers to the sixteenth-century singer Tansen, who was one of the nine 'jewels' in Emperor Akbar's darbar (or 'court'), and came to be known as 'Miyan Tansen'. Though facts to do with Tansen's genealogy are impossible to ascertain, the canonical story goes that he was born into a Hindu family as Ramtanu; the name Tansen was given to him by Akbar – it means 'king of the taan', a taan being a complex melodic pattern. A number of grandiose feats are attributed to Tansen, such as his lighting of the lamps in Akbar's court and bringing parched weather to the land by singing raga Deepak, and then – as citizens cried for relief from the heat – bringing rain and coolness by singing Megh Malhar. The little we know of his legacy, through three variations he's said to have created – Miyan ki Todi, Miyan ki Malhar, and Darbari – is, however, the opposite of grand or spectacular: it's subtle and exquisite. Admittedly, the first two came into existence well after Tansen's time; only Darbari, according to records, is reliably the historical Tansen's work. But if Tansen, real or otherwise, is one of the most powerful metaphors for composer or 'creator' in North Indian music, he remains instructive as to what, in the context of the raga, is meant by 'creation'.

Since we're looking at the Todi thaat here, I'll restrict myself to discussing Miyan ki Todi. When I say it was 'created' by Tansen, I don't mean he (or whoever it was that made the variation) brought it into existence from nothing. You can create a bandish, or composition, in a raga, but you can't compose a raga because ragas have no composers in the conventional sense – they are 'found' material turned into fluid and imperishable forms by the culture; once they become ragas, their inter-relationship of notes becomes the occasion for repeated interpretation and renewal in a way one wouldn't have previously thought possible. What Tansen did was intro-duce a modulation to Gujri Todi; he brought in the fifth glancingly, and in a specific counter-intuitive manner. Ordinarily, the fourth, ma, especially the sharp fourth, will lead to the calm and relief of the fifth, or pa. This linear ascent is exemplified by Bhatkande's thaat. Tansen won't have this. In Miyan ki Todi, the fifth is broached only after you've moved from the sharp fourth to the flat sixth; then, from the sixth you descend to the fifth and touch it briefly. You can't stay with it for more than a few seconds, according to the rules of Tansen's mod-ulation – in contravention of our time-worn expecta-tion that the fifth is an interval, the second most stable plateau after the tonic. No, Tansen, in Miyan ki Todi, must defamiliarise the fifth, make it rare, so that, even while it retains its calm, it's made transient, dream-like, its famous stability queried.

There's one more thing to be said about this raga. It's the way 'Tansen' assumes that there's an audience that will delight in this most slender of interventions.

'Slender', 'fine' – in Urdu, the word for these is 'bariq'. 'Bariqi' is part of the vocabulary of a culture that recognises the compelling nature of the slight, the frail.

9 Marwa
The notes in Bhatkande's thaat are:

sa <u>re</u> ga má pa dha ni

Though these notes are the same as raga Puriya Kalyan's, Bhatkande insists on calling the thaat 'Marwa'. In raga Marwa, unlike the thaat, there's no fifth note or pa. The raga's most unusual feature, though, is its sustained evasion of the tonic.

Marwa is an early-evening raga. Its opening movement might go like this:

sa
ni dha (lower octave)
dha ni <u>re</u> ga má dha (ascent from <u>re</u> into middle octave)
má dha má ga <u>re</u>
sa

The raga's main activity consists of a patient exploration of what's covered by the third and fourth lines above: the relationship of the sixth, dha, to <u>re</u>, the flat second. Not only is the homelike quality that the fifth gives to a scale absent from Marwa; its decision to abjure the tonic, sa, for as long as possible, gives it an inherent strangeness. The sa is the mooring of all ragas. Marwa's deliberately extended abstention from it is a radical spiritual experiment. Let loose from the tonic, returning repeatedly to re flat, a note neighbouring sa and yet infinitely distant from it, Marwa places itself voluntarily in limbo, choosing to become an exile from meaning as we generally experience it. Only at the end of each cycle of improvisation is it goaded back to the tonic; to the world as we know it.

10 The last of the major thaats is Bhairavi:

sa re ga ma pa dha ni sa

All notes that could possibly be flat are flat in this raga: re, ga, dha, ni – the second, third, sixth, and seventh. I should say here that the word used in Indian music for 'flat' – 'komal' – translates more accurately as 'soft'. 'Komal' eschews the implied straightness of flat because there are no straight notes in Indian music. Always arrived at by a glissando from a lower note, often touching the faintest trace of the next higher note first, anticipating at times through a wavering microtone the note to come, no note in Indian music except sa, the tonic, and pancham, the fifth, has a standalone existence. Each note, then, even the tivra or sharp notes, has a degree of softness or ambiguity. The word used to suggest this microtonal trembling has been, for millennia, 'shruti', a Sanskrit term also used of certain kinds of Vedic pronouncements. 'Shruti' is the overall conceptual precursor that encompasses later connoisseur-words like 'shukhya' or 'bariq', meaning 'subtle' or 'fine', that are in keeping with this tradition's cherishing of delicacy.

Bhairavi is rarely, if ever, subjected to a serious investigation in genres like khayal or dhrupad. It's a melody used in 'light classical' forms like thumri, and in devotionals. Although it's a morning raga, it's accorded a privilege no other raga is: it can be sung at any time, as long as it's performed at the end of a recital. This means that, if the vocalist sings a piece in Bhairavi, they're announcing the recital's end (no raga can be performed after it) not with finality but abandon, as if they and the audience were now on holiday from the time-specific rules that govern ragas, and had been released, at the concert's end, into a festive timelessness.

Unlike the Bhairavi thaat, the raga permits the occasional incorporation of the sharp fourth. You're also allowed to bring in natural versions of the flat notes. 'All twelve notes can be used in Bhairavi!' Govindji's brother-in-law Hazarilalji used to say, as if it were some kind of universal code or key.

So much for the thaats and the ragas they're related to.

In retrospect, it seems odd that Bhatkande didn't mention the pentatonic or five-note ragas as a separate category that was equally likely to comprise a pool of parent scales. The minor pentatonic ragas (Dhani and Malkauns) and the major one (Bhupali), not to mention other five-note ragas like Durga, Kalavati, Abhogi, and Megh, derive from folk melodies in India, Africa, and Europe. Their origins are as ancient as man, and, like man, these scales happen to be extant. Some of them have metamorphosed into other forms: the minor pentatonic is the blues and rock scale; you have the major pentatonic in rock and roll too, in songs like 'My Girl' and 'Mercedes Benz'. Long ago, a cultural shift turned these airs and tunes into some of North Indian classical music's most profound ragas, like Malkauns and Bhupali.

Bhatkande suggests that a raga like Malkauns derives from the Bhairavi thaat; but it seems doubtful that a minor pentatonic found the world over evolved from a seven-note melody. The emergence of the seven-note scale is, of course, itself a singular cultural occurrence. The earliest identifiable music theorist to record its existence is the shadowy Bharata (shadowy, as we know little about him), who predates Bhatkande by two millennia, and wrote his *Natya Shastra* ('Treatise on Performance') in Sanskrit in the second or third century BCE. In it, he classifies categories of aesthetic experience (*rasa*), and attempts to describe and pinpoint them.

Bharata also lists the seven notes or svaras, ascribing provenances to them. The names of the svaras in full are shadja (sa), which means 'that which gives birth to six' – that is, the other six notes; rishab (ri or re); gandhar (ga); madhyam (ma; from the same root as 'medium' or 'median'); pancham (or pa; from 'panch' or 'five'); dhaivat (dha); and nishad (ni). Bharata proposes the theory that each note is borrowed from an animal sound. So, sa came from the peacock's cry (I hear the upper tonic when I imagine this); rishab from the ox's lowing (this is a plausible and beautiful analogy for the second note; once the inner ear hears it, the other comparisons become audible); 'ga' from the goat's bleating; 'ma' from the krauncha bird or the demoiselle crane; pa from the cuckoo; dha from the horse's neigh; ni from the elephant's trumpeting.

These comparisons move me and make me smile. They also remind me of the wavering border, in the Hindustani tradition, not just between one note and another, but between music and existence – between sa and the peacock's cry. The raga is not a self-enclosed composition; it's an unfolding rather than a representation. We – whether we're listeners or performers – don't know it already as a piece to be performed. We listen to it as it happens. Listening takes us out of the control of authorship or ownership; it involves an openness to contingency. As in Bharata's account, music is a form of listening to the world.

I couldn't hear much from the twenty-fifth storey. I was too high up. I didn't know sound was absent from my life because it had been absent for such a long time. Before the twenty-fifth-storey flat, we'd lived for a decade on the twelfth storey. Again, there was that view of the Marine Drive. Again, there was that sense of removal. I don't mean the flat was silent. Hardly. For one thing, my mother would be singing or talking. She talked non-stop. I loved this even more about her than her music.

I was at sea – as an adolescent, and as an initiate. I was hardly going to college. As a sixteen-year-old, I'd partaken of Junior College for a year, and experienced short-lived glory when I won first prize in a competition in which the great Nandu Bhende, who'd played Judas in Alyque Padamsee's *Jesus Christ Superstar*, was the sole judge. I liked Nandu's Judas. I'd made sure that he received a copy of the words of my song, which was called 'Shout'. When I ascended the stage carrying my guitar and announced the name, people, after a second's flummoxed silence, began to heckle me, repeating loudly: 'Shout! Shout!' They shut up when I began to sing. Performing self-composed songs was, of course, unheard of, and I was stupid to embark on such an experiment: of writing songs, then daring to share them in what I knew would be a hostile environment. Nandu Bhende was studying my lyrics with a frown. This was because I'd forgotten them. Or it could have been because they were written in an obscure *Thick as a Brick* mode. Anyway, on stage, I was compelled to make up words instantaneously. We'd always made up sounds anyway when singing pop songs whenever the words escaped us: it wasn't difficult to reproduce American syllables. Now I was singing the words I remembered and substituting the rest with what sounded like English before an audience of two or three hundred. When I was done, the hecklers exploded with approval. This catapulted me to glory for part of that year. The girl who came close second, Amala Sheth, had sung the Carpenters' 'Only Yesterday' beautifully. We became friends for a while. My problem was that I grew bored of, and soon distanced myself from, what others admired in me. I lose faith very quickly. As a result, my life is full of fresh starts. I have few admirers, and the fault is partly mine: I can't be with my admirers for very long. I must change. The pattern began in 1978. By 1979, I was hardly going to college.

I spent a lot of time at home, like an invalid, or a child that won't go outside. Actually, I was out a lot, but by myself. I went for walks. I was bemused and captivated by the deadness of Cuffe Parade – the newly sprung tall buildings; the President Hotel; the clusters of concrete I'd seen from Malabar Hill, and which I was now in the middle of. I circled them, with the intensity of someone tracking down their double. Sometimes I went down a straight line and turned left, and walked and walked till I was in a Bombay I knew – the roundabouts and turns leading to Regal Cinema. Often, I found myself there in the evening. I'd walk past Elphinstone College as if unaware of what it was, spectating morbidly on drug dealers and prostitutes.

At home, I struggled to comprehend raga and tala; I was trying to discipline my voice. I'd sung the major scale for Govindji, and he'd observed to my mother with relief: 'He sings in tune.'

Now I had to expunge my sixteen-year-old's hint of tremolo. The sa must be steady and prolonged. The beginning was not only the first step. It was also the end. The sa was one's introduction, and surrender, to sur, or svara – words that mean note, melody, music. Unless the sa was engrossed in sur, one couldn't attempt the meends, the glissandos, that connect one note to another. The meend – an arc, or bent note – carries grace and movement. The voice that sings it needs to be assured in a way that's different from a voice producing voluble single notes. The meend isn't about loudness, or emphasis. Nor is it a cartilage joining two notes. It's an undulation – something ranging from a wave to a nuance.

Getting it right requires control. Before attempting the wave, you pause at the sa, deepening it.

I'd sung the major scale for Govindji in a straightforward way, in the way Julie Andrews had rendered 'Do, Re, Mi' in *The Sound of Music*. That is (with somewhat less conviction than Julie Andrews):

sa, re, ga, ma, pa, dha, ni, sa

then down again. By the comma, I don't mean a complete break between notes, but a regard for their separateness. I noticed that Govindji sang it differently:

sa (*ga* re) ga (*pa* ma) pa (*ni* dha) ni <u>sa</u>

sa ni dha pa ma ga re sa

Take the first two notes, sa, re, where I've coupled the second in parenthesis with the third note in italics: ga. I mean the sa glides to re with a hint first of leaping to ga, so that the re is arrived at on a tiny backward wave. Then re glides up to ga, and from ga glides up to ma, the fourth, by jumping over it to an intimation of pa, the fifth, before properly sounding the ma. And so on till the upper tonic. On the way down, Govindji slid back without a break, like a child descending a banister. Which is to say that Govindji made of the basic major scale

69

an aesthetic object that also captured an ethos in which notes aren't separate. His major scale wasn't 'made up' – it wasn't the sum – of seven notes; it was the unfolding, up and down, of an unbroken connection: the drawing out of a long moment.

In the way he sang sa re ga ma lay the key to achieving the incredibly complex embellishments and note-patterns that he executed with such (literally smiling) ease. Let's take a taan or note-pattern that's also pretty basic: the sapat. As the word suggests, it originates in the sa, goes up an octave, and comes down very fast. A sapat could be a major or minor scale, or a five-note one, but must traverse its journey through the octave at great speed, often on the syllable 'ah'. If I played it on the piano, each note would be independent of the others, however rapid the execution; the same's true of the guitar, if the scale were played up and down frets. It's only if you pull a string that you'd create a bent note, and get the undulation I'm referring to. A guitarist can usually produce one bent note at a time. A highly accomplished sitar player can produce four: that is, he or she can play, say, sa re ga ma by pulling a single string sideways rather than climbing the frets. This is difficult, but – as Indian musicians have demonstrated repeatedly – the impossible can be made possible. What drives one to an impossibility has to do with being possessed by desire – in this case, the desire is related to the sitar's ambition of replicating the human voice, its longing to sing. This is why schools of sitar-playing in the mid-twentieth century, in which complex bent notes dominated, came to be called the 'gayaki ang', or the 'singing style'. The singer has access neither to frets nor the pianist's keys: he produces the most difficult tonal effects, including the sapat, the fast up-and-down, not by coercion, but by pulling the string in his throat, by bending and stretching the sa significantly; as Govindji was, when he showed me in a leisurely way how the scale should be sung.

They say students of classical music practise for hours, and this must be true, because I had to. And I'd heard that classical singers begin at the age of six or seven (since the mythology is romantic, the age decreases, and the number of hours goes up); I felt inwardly at a disadvantage, like a person who's moved to a new country, tries to learn a new language, then write a novel in it, while other novelists there have of course known the language since they were born. My good fortune wasn't my talent (if I had any), but my parents. Despite misgivings, they stood by my idiosyncratic impulses. Part of my mother's doubts about me taking on Hindustani classical music was her knowledge of the effort involved, and her extreme concerns about my health. I'd had a congenital heart condition detected when I was three years old. In 1979, I went to America for the first time, where I was seen by a cardiologist in San Diego, where my cousin lived. He, unlike the doctors in Bombay I'd been seeing regularly for fourteen years, said I didn't need to be operated on till I was much older. My parents relaxed with this deferral of the inevitable. As Freud might have said, they admitted normal unhappinesses into their lives. On my return from America, I began to give most of my time to classical music. Doctors had dismissed the idea that rigorous practice had any relevance to a heart condition. My parents – maybe grateful for the certificate of life granted to the family – surrendered to my abstention from Junior College. Then I convinced my father that I'd drop out and start doing A and O levels from home, with a view to going to England to 'read' English. I'd never known a man like him; like a malingerer's best friend, he began to look for options that would make this possible. I started a correspondence course with Wolsey Hall, Oxford, to do A levels in English and – this was a concession to my father, who made no other request – Economics: if I failed as an artist, I would use my knowledge of Economics to get a job. I proceeded with my education – in this open-ended framework – without urgency. For hours, I aimed at fluency in sapat, and the vocal exercises Govindji had given me.

The word used for practice in North Indian classical music is 'riyaaz'. It and the word 'talim', for 'tutelage', are from Urdu, and a reminder of the preponderant impact, from the sixteenth century, of the Muslim ustad or virtuoso on the classical tradition. The Sanskrit precursor of 'riyaaz' would be 'sadhana', which refers to a long-term, perhaps lifelong, discipline whose end is not only a well-defined goal, but the pursuit of sadhana itself. In that sense, sadhana doesn't make a clear distinction between labour and its fruit, between preparation and performance.

Sadhana, unlike riyaaz, isn't a music-specific word; it could be used of football, or of living life itself.

Once you've entered the regime of riyaaz, you don't exit it easily. You may one day stop performing, but, if you're a classical musician, you don't stop burnishing or honing. Music is more akin to sport than to writing; inspiration counts for less than 'tayyari', the Urdu word for 'preparedness'. There's no spontaneity in the conventional sense: of bursting into songs as in Hindi films. The great singers who burst into song in cinema – like K. L. Saigal, Lata Mangeshkar, Asha Bhonsle, Mohammed Rafi, Kishore Kumar, Manna De, Talat Mahmood – had had, unlike the actors or characters they sang for, to do a lot of homework.

Riyaaz is the most secret part of yourself – the time you share with no one. You're listening to yourself: you're imperfect, as works-in-progress are. You're self-absorbed, like a bird, and, like a bird, vulnerable to the danger of being discovered. Being interrupted is akin to a bird's aloneness being shattered by movement. I've experienced this myself, and saw it in a woman practising for a performance of *The Pirates of Penzance* at Wolfson College in Oxford. The performance was to take place in the open air. She was warming up under a tree outside a room I was staying in for a few days. I kept very still, but moved slightly to hear her better. She didn't see me, but stopped abruptly and then, like a frightened animal, darted away and vanished.

Riyaaz, unlike performance, needn't be creative. It is self-imposed. But it shares with aesthetic production a kind of selflessness of investment. You do it to survive as an artist, independent of the appreciation you may or may not get. I saw this in my mother: the matter of regular practice even when few cared for her music. She continued her vocal exercises, her honing of interpretation, into her eighties, as long as she was physically able. I found myself thrown into this relentlessness in my late teens and early twenties. In London, in 1986, I stopped riyaaz only four days before my finals.

Riyaaz comprises a continuity in the creative self. Unlike our professional and conscious personas, which have an integrity, an identifiability, our creative selves are broken and self-estranging. You write a story or novel or poem; soon, you feel no attachment to it, and don't even know if it's any good. It's become inaccessible – as if the person who wrote it is a stranger. Of course, you act as if you still own the work, though the air of ownership is a pretence. Riyaaz is an intervention in the artist's feeling of discontinuity; it's what you must do every day, or every other day.

I say 'every other day' because it's important to take regular breaks from practice. You can't work your voice uninterruptedly any more than you can your imagination: both are prone to muscle fatigue. A jaded voice sounds similar to an underworked, unpractised one. Both find it difficult to execute the complexities that the voice in a perfect state of riyaaz can. The perfect state of riyaaz is a transient condition that we keep negotiating to hold on to. Very soon we discover that the aims of practice can't be attained through the will. You can't do a perfect sapat, for instance, by rushing the notes; you can't achieve the undulations of the gamak through force. Achieving these without force or determination involves technique, and sadhana.

Anyone partaking of the arts must partake of riyaaz. Art is an acquired taste: our first experience of it is foreign, our approach to it sceptical. Over time, we may begin to take pleasure in it. This process – of outgrowing resistance and beginning to savour – is a kind of riyaaz.

My father spent a lot of time in the office those days. He also had to fly frequently to Delhi – India was about a decade from deregulation, and companies needed permission regularly from civil servants.

I wrote poetry: I began to learn a bit of Bengali – part of my gradual self-scripted education in Bengali and Indian culture. It was as if I was neither at home nor at university, but in a retreat where I was allowed to do these things.

'In the room the women come and go' – my mother and father came and went; and, a few times a week, Govindji, his brother-in-law Hazarilalji, and his brother Girdharji, who played the tabla, arrived for 'sittings'.

With the music came the words, of songs.
Let me take a composition at random:

> umad ghumad aye
> kare kare badara
>
> bijuri chamakat
> meha barasat
> piya parades chhaye

This is a khayal in raga Megh. The composition, in the ten-beat jhaptaal, is probably by my teacher's father, Laxman Prasad Jaipurwale. Here's a basic translation:

> Umad ghumad, they come:
> black, black clouds.
>
> Lightning flashes.
> It starts to rain.
> My beloved's abroad.

'Umad ghumad' is onomatopoeic: words for thunder in Avadhi or Braj bhasha, variants of Hindi in which the songs – classical, folk, and devotional – of the North Indian tradition are written.

For me, words like these produced a sensation that had a lightning-like suddenness. First, there was the economy: the lyrics aren't even descriptive; they're a terse bringing-together of characteristics. This paucity felt right.

Then there's the language: Avadhi. It's a literary language in which the words of khayal, the 'light classical' thumri, and bhajan (or the devotional) are composed; yet it's also a spoken language, the tongue which locals in Bihar and Uttar Pradesh use even today. It's to be distinguished from another version of Hindi: the standard version or 'khari boli' – literally, 'upright speech'. Khari boli is urban and official: it's the national language.

Avadhi is a dialect and a language that began to be used for literary purposes from around the fourteenth century. By the end of the nineteenth century, with the emergence of literary modernity, it was supplanted by an animated, urbane variant of khari boli called 'Hindustani': a mix of Hindi and Urdu. But there are no khari boli lyrics in khayals or thumris; they're in Avadhi. Hindi film songs are mainly in Hindustani: they're completely of the city. A few simple comparisons: when in khari boli you say 'karta' for 'do', a rural North Indian will use the word 'karat'. When in khari boli you say 'jata' for 'to go', Avadhi has the affectionate, intimate-sounding 'jawat'. In society, the first has associations of correctness; the second of the rustic. Not so in khayal, in which Avadhi expresses grandeur and intimacy equally. It's steeped in love – of the world, of the beloved, and of the divine.

What's history – that is, tradition; our human inheritance? Is it already there for us to find? If so, do we
acquaint ourselves with it through study?

For the Romans two millennia ago, history was death:
a domain populated with great and ordinary personages
from the past. You didn't piece the past together as if it
was over; you encountered it, like Aeneas did when he
entered Hades. Dante, in the thirteenth century, adopts
the same vocabulary of discovery; he doesn't seek out
the world of the dead, but comes to it after taking a
wrong turn. In hell, his former mentor, Brunetto Latini,
on being approached by Dante, asks:

> What brings you here before your day?
> Is it by accident, or Providence?
> Who is this man who guides you on your way?
>   (trans. Robert Lowell)

'This man', as we know, is Virgil, who shows to Dante
that the past is to be arrived at without premeditation,
and met with, face to face.

> I answered, 'In the world that lies serene
> and shining over us, I lost my path,

even before the first young leaves turned green.
Yesterday morning when my steps had come
full circle, this man appeared . . .'

Tagore's Virgil was the fourth-century Sanskrit poet
Kalidasa. But – in contrast to Virgil and Dante – Kalidasa
didn't physically accompany Tagore as he revisited history: that is, the fourth-century Ujjain in which Kalidasa
had lived. Tagore went to it through the form of trans-
port we call 'reading'. He read Kalidasa's long poem
Meghaduta; then, in 1889, he wrote a poem called
'Meghdut' about reading Kalidasa's poem. Meghdut literally means 'cloud-messenger'. In Kalidasa's poem, a
lover asks a cloud to carry with it a message from him
to his loved one, who lives in the city of Alaka. The long
poem describes the lover's imagining of the cloud's journey. The cloud, in other words, has become, as it was
for Wordsworth (who may well have read Kalidasa in
William Jones's translation), a figure for the imagination; and the imagination makes present to us, through
anticipation, what's absent.

Tagore shows us, in his late-nineteenth-century poem,
how reading the *Meghaduta* takes him, cloud-like, to
Kalidasa's world a thousand years ago. Unlike Dante and
Virgil in the *Inferno*, neither Tagore nor Kalidasa is cor-
poreally present in that world: yet they're brought closer
to each other through the act of reading, which is animated by longing, or desire, imagination's other name.

Reading Kalidasa makes Tagore 'lose his path' in the known world. He is elsewhere. Like Dante, he can inhabit this place – call it Ujjain; or Hades; or history – only for a limited time. The spell ends when he finishes reading Kalidasa's poem; Tagore records the abruptness with which he comes back to the room in which he's sitting.

Tagore was gripped by the thought of arriving at history by chance, through a turn in the road. In 'Swapna' or 'Dream', which I think of as his companion piece to 'Meghdut', and which he wrote in 1897, he describes by what means, and why, he revisits the past:

> Far very far away
>   in the kingdom of dreams, in Ujjain,
> I can't recall when, I'd gone to look by the river Sipra
> for my first love from a previous life.
> Lodhra-pollen on her face, the lotus of creation
> in her hands, kunda buds on the ears, kurubak blossoms
> in her hair, body ensconced in blood-red cloth,
> the anklets on her feet only half-audible.
>   One spring day
> I'd painstakingly traced the long way back.
>
> (my translation)

As he begins to find his way, it grows dark, and he phrases his progress in terms that recall Dante's opening: 'My beloved's house / was on a narrow bent path, unfrequented, remote'. In Longfellow's translation, the *Inferno* begins: 'Midway upon the journey of our life / I found myself within a forest dark, / For the straight-forward pathway had been lost.' I don't think Tagore is deliberately echoing Dante; he never cites the latter's impact on him, as he does certain English poets', like Chatterton's and Shelley's. But there's a pattern being repeated here, of how certain poets and artists move towards history without prior preparation. Tagore's speaker in 'Swapna' differs from Dante and Aeneas in one way; his first love from his 'previous love' and he can't be interlocutors; though he's back in Ujjain, he can't remember its language:

> . . . taking my hand in hers,
> eyes kind, she softly asked only this:
> 'O friend, I trust you're well?' Gazing on her face
> I started to speak, but had nothing to say.
> I'd forgotten that tongue. We thought hard and tried
> to summon each other's names, but they'd gone.
> So much we considered as we stared at each other,
> unstoppable tears falling from blinking eyes!

The path I'd taken from air guitarist to pop musician to Canadian singer-songwriter to Indian classical vocalist involved a journey, in which the last was a turn, a straying off, an inadvertent wandering, until I was where I hadn't expected to be. I was close to history. The raga and the Avadhi language were my points of contact with a 'previous life'. I could be *there* only for a short while. Then I'd be back again, in Cuffe Parade, on the twenty-fifth storey.

Govindji was hardly Virgil. He had his own journey to make, between two worlds – the rich ladies of Cuffe Parade and Malabar Hill and the young aspirational singers in the suburbs; and the exquisite compositions of the Kunwar Shyam gharana (literally, 'family'), of which he was the only great living exponent. Maybe he required a Virgil too; or, even more, patrons. My guide was really Hazarilalji. He played the harmonium and the tabla. He was a teacher of kathak dance. He knew the ragas and talas. He acted as if he had time on his hands.

Just as I'd been a Canadian singer-songwriter, I became, for a while, an Avadhi poet. I began to compose devotionals – the effect of my getting to know Meerabai, Kabir, Tulsidas, Surdas, and a poet I'd never heard of before – Chandrasakhi – whose songs my teacher sang. I didn't imitate them. I became their contemporary, as I'd been Joni Mitchell's contemporary, and Neil Young's.

My mother – in fact, everyone around me – withstood my susceptibility to being now one thing, now another. My abnormal phases were nothing compared to those of the bhakti poets'. My phases passed. Abnormality defined their lives.

Meera, or Meerabai, is probably the most popular of the *bhakti* or devotional poets. She lived from 1498 to 1556, but her life is part myth, and part of the myth is her own creation. I certainly didn't know these dates when I first began to listen seriously to her songs in 1978, sung by my mother and her teacher. The songs are the principal source of her mythology. Meera was a mystical-romantic-confessional poet, in that she and her love of Krishna, and the numerous impediments to that love, were her subject. She wrote simply – when I say 'she', I mean the historical personage called 'Meera', as well as others who wrote songs ascribed to her. Hazarilalji dismissed her words for lacking individuality: '*Paga ghungru bandh Meera nachi re* – is this poetry?' (The words mean, 'Tying ghungrus to her feet, Meera dances'.) A word on Hazarilalji: he was semi-literate. Yet he was the product of a literary culture. Poetry, for him, meant compression: a kind of inner pressure, shaping the sound of words, which he found in Tulsidas but not in Meera. I say this because, based on what I came to know of Hazarilalji and bhakti poets, it would be wrong to think that verbosity is a characteristic of orality, and precision an expectation created by literacy. Although the songs were more sung than read for Hazarilalji, he had a clear-eyed preference for a beauty that arose not from emotion but from language.

As with many confessional poets, Meera is known to millions for her life story as much as she is for her lines. While I agree with Hazarilalji that there's an unresistant quality to her diction, I still think she left behind a compelling episodic account of her life and her out-of-control but joyous besottedness with Krishna. She's said to have been born to an aristocratic family in Kurki, Rajasthan. She fell in love with Krishna as a child and chose him as her bridegroom. Most of us graduate from make-believe objects of adoration to real ones, and from real ones to those we can make a life with; Meera belongs to the tiny minority who don't. Krishna – or Hari, or Govind, or Giridhar Nagar, names by which she called him – was her one husband. This was no doubt infuriating to her family, who, however devout they were, would have had the ability to distinguish between fact and fiction, and profane and religious love. Meera had little time for such distinctions: they fell away before her. Perhaps her unrelenting nature – the songs self-consciously portray one who's passionate and obstinate – made it hard for her family to get her married. Historical records suggest she married Bhoj Raj, the prince or Rana of Mewar, at the age of eighteen – late, for a woman of her era. In her songs, Meera (or those who wrote in her name) casts her husband and his family as the enemy. She refers to him not as swami, or 'lord' ('prabhu', meaning the same thing, is reserved for Hari), but coldly as 'Rana'. Contrary to popular assumptions, though, her husband, the Rana, was actually protective of his strange wife, and it was only after his death that she was really vulnerable to his family's malice. It's very possible that 'Rana' refers not to Meera's husband, but to the brother who succeeded him after his death.

Meera knew she was an embarrassment. She celebrated this fact with melancholy bravado: 'log kahe Meera bhai bawri' – 'People say Meera's crazy.' Meera uses 'log' (or 'people') with realism: she means by it a society with a low tolerance for spiritual abandon. Her figure for abandon is dance: 'Tying ghungrus to her feet, Meera dances' – the line that did little for Hazarilalji and voices her resolve to affirm her oddity.

87

Even more than 'log', it's the husband's family that enacts society's animosity to spiritual love. The line that follows 'log kahe Meera bhai bawri' is 'saas kahe kul nasi re' – 'People say Meera's crazy / her mother-in-law says she's destroyed the lineage.' The Rana's family tries to kill her twice: once, by sending her a serpent in a box; and another time as she sang, 'vish ka pyala Rana ne bheja / pi gayi Meera hasi re' – 'Rana sent a cup of poison / Meera drank it, laughing.' Meera, or whoever the author of this 'Meera bhajan' is, addresses the Rana with the mock-intimate 'meré' or 'my' – 'meré Ranaji'; 'my Lord' – while making it clear who her actual lord is:

> O my Ranaji
> I sing Govind's praises!
> If the king gets angry, I can flee the country.
> Where to go
> if I anger Hari?
>
> Sent a box
> with a black snake in it
> I took it for
> a shaligram.
>
> Rana sent
> a cup of poison.
> I drank it up
> like amrit.

Meerabai
is mad with love.
I've found myself
a dark husband.

The innocence and audacity of the last declaration –
'Meerabai prem diwani'; 'Meerabai / is mad with love'
– is near impossible to translate. 'Shaligram' is a stone or
fossil revered as a holy object; 'amrit' (literally, 'death-
less') is divine elixir; 'dark husband' is an expression
of Meera's sudden brimming, after her mocking litany
against the Rana, with affection for her 'sanwariya var',
the dark-skinned Krishna (the Rana, a high-caste Rajput,
would have been fair). Dark is secret and close; 'sanwariya', in Avadhi, means both 'dark' and 'lover'. In Bengali,
the corruption of 'shyamala', derived from 'sanwariya',
fortuitously sounds identical to 'sheola', the word for
'moss', or 'moss-green'. The word 'Hari' is linked to
'hara', Hindi for 'green'. Krishna is very dark, which is
why he's blue in paintings. He's a cowherd. This folk
version of Krishna finds its full-bodied literary incarnation in the *Bhagavat Purana* (from the tenth century).
Part of Krishna's power – over his devotees, over the
women who love him, beginning with Radha, who too
had a husband – lies in the signal he sends out through
his music. Krishna plays the flute: to those who hear it,
the sound is distracting; it brings to a stop what they're
doing. In the words of a thumri Govindji taught me:

murli wale shyam
kahe ko bajaye re

tero murli mero
mana har lino
bisraya sab kaam

Or:

Why must you play these notes
O flute-playing Shyam?

Your flute's
won my heart,
it's made me forget my work.

Krishna is a reminder of what listening does; how it takes us out of ourselves. We read novels, as Walter Benjamin said, to find ourselves in them; we listen to be elsewhere.

One of Meera's songs that caught my attention – I later composed a melody for it, in my early twenties, combining ragas Miyan ki Malhar and Gaud Malhar – was 'barse bundiyan sawan ki' ('sawan's raindrops fall'). It captures her joys in the midst of her solitude. Meera's joys are to do with the imagination, which, as I've said, is synonymous with desire. Desire, if it's intense enough, can produce four consecutive notes on a pulled sitar string; it can bring Hari back to you. 'Wanting' something creates its own reality; it makes the rules of what we ordinarily think plausible irrelevant. Here are the song's opening couplets:

> barse bundiya sawan ki
> sawan ki mana bhawan ki
>
> sawan me umangiyo mero mana
> bhanak suni Hari awan ki

Or:

> Sawan's raindrops fall
> heart-gladdening drops of sawan

In sawan my heart leaps up
I've heard a rumour Hari's coming

Sawan is the wettest month in North India. It starts in the middle of July. Summer's particularly parched in Rajasthan, where Meera lived. By mid-May, the rains are awaited with desperation. Meera does something clever. She conflates the yearning for rain, common to much of India, with her desire for Hari. The rains grip the Indian imagination not just because they're much needed, but because they involve the intervention of elsewhere. Everything about them is figurative: the first breeze; the drop in temperature; black clouds and downpour. All these, like Hari, are harbingers of unfamiliarity. Indians imagine the rain because they long for it; even the shock of getting drenched doesn't reduce its fictionality.

Poor Meera! Isolated by her husband's family, seized by an incomprehensible compulsion! I learnt about a variety of spiritual desires at the time, just as I was possessed by my own. From Bhimsen Joshi's rendition of a bhajan by Brahmanand, I grew conscious of an ambition that was shocking yet compelling. The bhajan begins: 'jo bhaje Hari ko sada / so hi param pada payega' – 'Whoever meditates always on Hari / will get the supreme reward.' What reward? Property; happiness; heaven? The answer comes towards the end: 'phir janam nahi ayega' – 'then you won't have to be born' – the incentive declared without overt excitement. On hearing it, the seventeen-year-old self's ears pricked up.

Meera had her own modulation on the matter of 'janam', or being born. She's said to be the author of these lines:

> janam janam ki bana lo dasi
> janam janam guna gawungi

That is:

> Let me be your servant birth after birth
> In birth after birth I'll sing your praises

For Meera, the trauma of existence and the prospect of returning to the world repeatedly was offset by the experience of bhakti, or love: evidently enough compensation for the mixed bag life is. Not for her Brahmanand's 'param pada'. For 'Where can we live but days?', as Larkin asked. 'They come, they wake us / Time and time over. / They are to be happy in.' Meera phrases the question differently: 'How, except through being born, can we love Hari?'

For me, at the age of seventeen (and even now), these interrogations, to do with the impulse to return to life or, on the other hand, to escape it, seemed more immediate and to cut deeper than Western thought's academic pre-occupation with free will and predestination.

In Hindi songs, even in films, the word 'janam' occurs in a pair – 'janam janam'; 'birth after birth' – to suggest eternity. Where an English pop song will say, 'I'll love you forever', a Hindi film song will claim, 'janam janam tujhe chahunga', meaning the same thing. 'Forever' is not static, immutable; it comprises a journey through lifetimes of companionship. For Meera, adoration of Hari is the thread through which successive lifetimes are strung, bead-like.

I continued to do riyaaz – the paltas or vocal exercises Govindji had given me. 'Palta rataana' – the second word means 'to do again and again'; it's used of parrots too – a form of memorising and repetition. Govindji began teaching me ragas Bilawal and Bhupali. A khayal composition is different from a bhajan in the way classical music is different from devotional music, though classical singers will have bhajans in their repertoire, and often end their recital with the romantic semi-classical form called the thumri, or a bhajan, or both. A khayal – whether it's a drut fast-tempo composition or a vilambit slow-tempo one – has two verses, both usually couplets; or two lines in the first verse, three in the second. As with the bhajan and ghazal (the Urdu love song), the rhyme structure is aa and ba, although the ghazal/bhajan will extend this by several couplets – aa, ba, ca, da, ea – improvising on the opening rhyme. The tune of the first couplet, which is called 'sthayi' ('mooring') in the khayal, is set to the lower and middle registers of the raga. The second couplet is the 'antara', the interior; here the melody rises to the upper tonic and completes the octave. The bhajan's melody moves in the same way, but its aim is not to explore the tonal journey from sa to **sa.** Instead, it unfolds, like the ghazal,

95

in couplet after couplet, riffing on its subject: the love of Krishna, or Hari, or Ram. Although the two-verse composition of the khayal may be addressed, or have references, to Hari, its ambition, within the space provided by those two lines and the space provided by the tala, is to approach the raga's progression on various levels. Words are everything in a ghazal or bhajan; in the khayal, they may be mumbled, as if their only use was to return to the tala's one. Words in khayal become sound; referentiality is given a grudging secondary status. The phoneme becomes a function of raga and tala rather than of meaning. It's as if the khayal won't subscribe to a conventional notion of text; the boundaries that delineate text as text, and make a song recognisable as 'song', are dispensed with. (This, I suspect, is not the case with Carnatic music, where both devotional content and 'sahitya', or textual content, have greater centrality.) The tendency of some khayal singers to maul words baffles audiences accustomed mainly to bhajans and ghazals, who wish to understand and be moved by what they hear. The seeming indifference in khayal to communication – to, in literary-journalistic jargon, 'accessibility' – I associate with its development as a modernist form.

Yet bhajans introduced me to the culture's emotional core. I became an Avadhi poet and composed – contemporaneously with composing folk-rock songs on the guitar – two or three Hindi devotionals. All my songs were love songs then; I moved between profane and sacred love as unselfconsciously as I did between American English ('my baby') and Avadhi. Anyway, Meera and other bhakti poets had already shown that – at least in India – there's no reliable demarcation between loving a human or a god. What's certain is that you don't expend romantic energy on your husband; whether god or human, it's usually someone else. Both in the bhajan and the thumri – a leisurely, semi-classical form that was refined in Wajid Ali Shah's court in the eighteenth century – the speaker in the song, irrespective of the poet's or the performer's gender, is a woman: often it's Radha, a married woman, yearning for Krishna, worrying about her sister-in-law or mother-in-law waking up at the sound of her anklets when she goes out to see him at night. One might hazard a distinction between the romantic song, whether it's a ghazal or a pop song, and the bhajan. The first is mostly about unrequited love, while bhakti is an illicit passion. It's curious that the Victorian-era penal code in India still sees adultery as a crime, while the spiritual condition of the Hindu devotee is an adulterous one. The only instance that comes readily to mind in Western culture of the sort of disruption Krishna causes, not only to the female soul (and all souls, according to those who view Vaishnav mythology as allegory, are female) but to the family, is Pasolini's *Teorema*. The Hollywood Western *Shane* too has a blond stranger riding into the homestead, exciting the wife's affection and the children's wonder, bringing new meaning to the family's life in the far-flung outback, but receding before sexual tension and turbulence develop. I've always found the closeness of 'Shane' to 'Shyam', one of Krishna's most beloved names (meaning 'the dark one'), fortuitous. In *Teorema*, though, the arrival of the young, sexy Terence Stamp (only ever referred to as 'the visitor') has an extraordinary effect on a bourgeois family. He spends a short duration with them: rescues the maid from her temptations towards suicide; sleeps with, and brings sexual satisfaction to, the wife; seduces the son; has a close relationship with the daughter; tends to the sick and ailing husband; then, abruptly, he vanishes. The departure causes a sea-change. The maid goes back to her village, becoming a mystic who performs miracles; finally, she immolates herself in a spiritual ecstasy. The daughter goes into a coma. The son leaves home in his quest to become an artist. The mother cruises the roads in her car, seeking transient sexual encounters. The father divests himself of both his clothes and material assets – his business – and goes off into the wilderness. Only *Teorema*, in the Western imagination, conceives an upheaval – at once sexual and religious – caused by a visitor that's worthy of Meera. Some said the film was about Christ, like Pasolini's *The Gospel According to St Matthew*; but that was not the Vatican's view. When the film won the International Catholic Jury grand award, it 'attacked the award in an official statement', as Roger Ebert points out.

There's another distinction between the love song and the devotional, which I've already hinted at. When I wrote folk-rock songs and sang them with my guitar, I upbraided my addressee – a non-existent woman whose non-existence didn't diminish my agonising over her – for letting me down: I sang as a man. In the bhajans, I occupied – without realising it – Radha's vantage-point. I did both without any sense of conflict.

Why did I write those bhajans? I don't know. It's not like I had a 'religious turn' – I'm not even sure what that means. It's as if Avadhi allowed me to access a new emotion. You'll notice your personality changes marginally when you switch languages, or even if you jokingly adopt an accent. One part of you closes down while fresh possibilities present themselves. Something similar happened to me: not just a cultural transformation, but a recovery of history from inside the self, rather than from outside it. History is a loss of the self you know: the one that speaks in the language and accent it grew up with, and was educated in. Tagore dramatises this in his short story 'Khudito Pashan', 'The Hungry Stones', which he wrote in 1895 after staying at a Mughal palace in Gujarat, where his older brother Satyendranath was posted as a civil servant. The colonial era was in place; four centuries of Mughal rule had faded like a dream at daybreak. In Tagore's story, Srijut, a Bengali tax collector, begins, on moving to such a mansion, to imperceptibly lose himself. During the day he's in his usual sola hat and jacket; at night, he takes on the style of the Muslim aristocracy while awaiting a mysterious presence, a woman:

> I would then be transformed into some unknown personage of a bygone age, playing my part in unwritten history; and my short English coat and tight breeches did not suit me in the least. With a red velvet cap on my head, loose *pyjamas*, an embroidered vest, a long flowing silk gown, and coloured handkerchiefs scented with *attar*, I would complete my elaborate toilet, sit on a high-cushioned chair, and replace my cigarette with a many-coiled *nargilah* filled with rose-water, as if in eager expectation of a strange meeting with the beloved one.

'Khudito Pashan' is sometimes called a 'ghost story'. It's also a historical story, except that it conceives history not as a particular period, but as a haunting.

What I found exceptional in the devotionals was their tone. Whoever the elusive addressee – Hari, or Ram, or some nameless recipient of devotion – the bhajan resisted apportioning blame. It's not as if the devotee had deceived themselves into thinking that the god, or happiness, would one day be theirs. They were clear-eyed about the fact that yearning and separation comprised a continual state, but chose to discreetly overlook the disappointment that devotion brings. Instead, the human decides to efface themselves and praise the object of affection, where praise involves a kind of overlooking, a patience (both of which are manifestations of love), as well as a subtle reprimand. I think this is true, for example, of 'tu dayalu deen haun' by Tulsidas:

> You're the kind one;
> I'm destitute.
>
> You give:
> I'm the beggar.
>
> I'm the one
> that's caught in sin.

You vanquish sin
with virtue.

The more a bhajan praises, the more it seems to shield
from blame; the reproach is implicit, and inseparable
from an affection which is finally indifferent to God's
shortcomings: it knows them, and ignores them.

Around the age of eighteen or nineteen I discovered
Hopkins, and the tone of one sonnet, of subdued imprecation to do with the beloved's unfairness, reminded me
of the patience exhibited by bhakti poetry:

Thou art indeed just, Lord, if I contend
With thee; but, sir, so what I plead is just.
Why do sinners' ways prosper? and why must
Disappointment all I endeavour end?
    Wert thou my enemy, O thou my friend
How wouldst thou worse, I wonder, than thou dost
Defeat, thwart me?

'Wert thou my enemy, O thou my friend' recalls Tulsidas's
antinomies ('You give: / I'm the beggar'); Hopkins is
more candid in his complaint, but Tulsidas's refusal to
accuse has an equal resonance.

The other work that felt close to a bhakti poem at
the time was Bob Dylan's 'Don't Think Twice, It's All
Right'. I wasn't an admirer; but the song held me. I
reacted against Dylan's persona, his flamboyance, his

hectoring; but there's a note of imprecation in his song-writing, from this song to 'It Ain't Me Babe' ('No, no, it ain't me babe / It ain't me you're looking for') to 'Like a Rolling Stone' and 'Idiot Wind' ('You're an idiot, babe'), which I associate with his mysticism. I first heard this most powerfully in 'Don't Think Twice, It's All Right':

> Still I wish there was somethin' you would do or say
> To try and make me change my mind and stay
> We never did too much talkin' anyway
> But don't think twice, it's all right

Here's an object of love who's unfathomable, who provokes love and speech while being slow to reciprocate with speech or love themselves, but who's familiar enough to open up to; even, in Dylan's case, be rude with. Yet, the next moment, comes the placatory note, making, in a way, the beloved unimportant: 'But don't think twice, it's all right'. Tulsidas's 'tu dayal deen hau' ('You're the kind one; / I'm destitute') is also a way of saying: 'It's OK; your words and view of things don't, in the end, matter: only my love for you does.' 'Tohe mohe naate anek,' Tulsidas notes in the last verse, 'maniye jo mane' – 'You and I are related in many ways, / Acknowledge whichever one you wish'; as if God were irrelevant to the relationship's veracity. 'I gave her my heart but she wanted my soul,' sings Dylan; then concludes, 'I ain't sayin' you treated me unkind / You could have done better but I don't mind / You just kinda wasted my precious time'; and then again shifting the tone, 'But don't think twice, it's all right' – summing up the dilemma of bhakti, of giving oneself ('my precious time' is a euphemism for 'life') to what one loves but doesn't understand; then rising above the source of hurt. Bhakti isn't about God; it's about the impracticality and dignity of human emotion.

Despite the fact that it expressed unrequited adoration, the bhajan – along with the raga, and the Indian miniatures of the sixteenth, seventeenth, and eighteenth centuries – introduced me to a universe without tragedy. In that sense, it wasn't, strictly speaking, a *moral* universe. Tragedy creates meaning. I grew up thinking that pain assigns significance: that what was painless was trivial. That was *my* moral universe, and, I think, many others'. Now I found a culture that had cast aside this position as if it were an anachronism. But how to describe the overhaul involved in deriving value not from tragedy, but joy? Tragedy is a culmination; but what *is* joy? It's not easy to pinpoint, because it's not contained in an episode of importance; it's a participation in existence, with no separate definition for itself. It's everywhere, and its lack of outline makes it difficult to identify. Its strength is that it can reside in the tiniest and most unresistant of things – a grain of rice or a strand of hair. This is why a Mughal or Kangra miniature can contain more life, more of the cosmos, than a huge Renaissance painting.

I'd grown up with the notion – given to me by my education, and books I'd read and films I'd watched – that life was about gathering experience, and consequently becoming wise. Then, out of school, doing A levels by myself, I began to become aware of the raga and its relationship to the present moment.

It was at this time that I had a pointless argument with a man much older than me about William Blake's *Songs of Innocence and Experience*. He was a friend of the father of a friend of mine. I didn't know him. Yet, suddenly, we were in the middle of a disagreement. I said that Blake must have written the songs of innocence *after* the songs of experience, rather than in the order in which they'd been placed in the book. It wasn't true, but it suited me to say it might be. I wasn't so much arguing with the man as a certain idea of chronology and development we all subscribed to. The man was irritated, and asked me to explain. I said: 'You only arrive at the simplicity and calm of innocence *after* experience, not before it.' I now no longer know what I meant; but the need to reverse the order was fresh and obstreperous. I wouldn't have made that remark if I hadn't been touched by Indian art's sloughing off of mortality and death; its fruition in life. Innocence is the fruit of experience, it seemed to say. If that's the case, we don't have to concern ourselves with a proper 'ending' in the narrative sense; we stay with the beginning, as the khayal does with alaap.

The precedence that deferral takes in India's cultural imagination, in bhakti, in Kalidasa's *Meghaduta*, over union and completion finds its tonal counterpart especially in a dimension of the note that's said to be peculiar to Indian music: the shruti.

The shruti is not a form of magic or yoga; it's the engendering, within the raga, of multiple, oscillating, microtonal leading notes. In Western music, the leading note is the seventh note of the major scale, ti (ni in Indian music). If you sing the notes, you'll find that you can't stop at ti; it strains for the tonic – that is, do. To stop at ti is to feel a frustrated incompleteness. Maybe this is why Julie Andrews called ti 'a drink with jam and bread', a makeshift meal before dinner at day's end.

In the raga, every note *can* be a leading note, anticipating the next note by briefly occupying a state of suspension in which the specific note is clearly sounded, but is also agitated by a wave that measures less than a semitone. The shruti is not a random stirring; that is, it's not the equivalent of putting your finger in a pool of water and stroking it absent-mindedly. It's a gradation you have to hear, and then produce. It's not to be confused with vibrato: its aim is not to express your heart. That kind of self-expression, which the vibrato came to represent after romanticism, is anathema to Indian classical music. Shruti has to do with the note's anticipation of the next note, as well as its refusal to be immediately transformed into it. It's to do with sometimes preferring a state of becoming, of *being* transformed, to full transformation and resolution. The journey's end is important; but the journey itself has precedence. The journey – *badhat*; progression – is another term for delay.

I was demonstrating the *raison d'être* of shruti by singing the notes of Purvi to a friend, the pianist John Kamfonas. He mentioned Cavafy's 'Ithaka'. I went home and reread the poem, wondering if he'd been thinking of these lines:

> Keep Ithaka always in your mind.
> Arriving there is what you're destined for.
> But don't hurry the journey at all.
> Better if it lasts for years,
> so you're old by the time you reach the island . . .
> (trans. Edmund Keeley)

Which brings me to the meend – the glissando, or glide, or bent note. At this point, I'd like only to make an observation about the distance it covers. The shortest distance a meend traverses is the smallest unit on the twelve-note scale: the semitone. A semitone is what separates a note from its closest neighbour: ni (or ti) from the tonic sa (or do); sa from re flat; re flat from re natural. The widest span a meend covers in a raga is usually an octave, from, say, the lower to the upper tonic; it could go further.

Distance is made peculiarly equitable by the meend; that is, nearness and far-apartness are shown to be constructs. The voice, when singing a meend between ni and sa (a semitone), can seem to cover a tonal register, a range, equal to a meend stretching from sa to pa, the fifth: eight semitones. Mastery of meend can create unexpected room between notes we know are neighbours.

Despite the deadness surrounding the twenty-fifth-storey flat, music made me notice the universe: the sun, diffuse, on the left, and automobiles advancing on the right, on Marine Drive. Early evening. I'd think of words I'd picked up from khayal compositions: 'bhavsagar' – 'the ocean of earthly existence'. It was a new idea to me, but it made sense in Cuffe Parade, where featureless water extended endlessly on the left. The line from the drut khayal I'd heard my teacher sing was 'bhavsagar dukha apare' – 'the ocean of earthly existence is sorrow without a shore'. In the midst of the journey, you sing, according to the lyric, Hari's name: 'gao re Hari ke bhajan'. The thought was a bit terrifying at seventeen: that life has no solid foundation; that, like an expanse of water, it has no clear ending or outline – you're simply adrift.

During the monsoons, when lines of rain marched towards our building, I'd sing raga Miyan ki Malhar. There was little beauty to the rains in Cuffe Parade, but I didn't want to miss the opportunity.

I had in mind the legend of Miyan Tansen, Akbar's principal court musician, lighting lamps in the darbar through the heat produced by his rendition of raga Deepak (no one sings this raga now; it literally means 'lamp' or 'light'), and then bringing relief by singing raga Megh Malhar, making it rain. There's more than one version of this story, but there's always a downpour at the end. The word 'Malhar' is synonymous with 'monsoon raga'. Raga Malhar isn't performed today – one isn't even sure what it is – but all monsoon ragas except Megh are largely variations of Malhar: Gaud Malhar, Megh Malhar, Sur Malhar, Meerabai Malhar, Jayant Malhar, Ramdasi Malhar, Nat Malhar, and Tansen's own Miyan ki Malhar. These variations point to an aesthetic of constant reinterpretation. The monsoons appear to provoke reworking: as if extant ragas must be inevitably transformed by the rains.

I thought it would be fun to see if I could make it rain. So, at the end of June (the official inaugural date for the monsoon being 10 June), or in July or August, I'd pick up my tanpura and go to the drawing room and start singing Sadarang's vilambit composition in Miyan ki Malhar, 'Kareem naam tero' – 'Kareem is your name.' If it was raining when I started, I'd notice it stopped a few minutes later. If it was overcast, the rains refused to come during the length of the exposition. Sometimes it rained in a burst when I sang a non-monsoon raga like Bhupali. My experiences with Malhar were non-mythic, non-miraculous.

*

Despite the legend, I find the culture – musical, spiritual – is less interested in miracles than in life. The rains are an outburst of existence. You acknowledge them by singing a Malhar; and, by acknowledging them, you add another dimension of veracity to them: as D. H. Lawrence said of Cézanne's apples, they aren't true to life, they're '*more true to life*'. This is what one means by 'making it rain': a bringing to existence, rather than a miracle in the conventional sense.

I recall having a conversation with Hazarilalji about the devotional poets. We turned to the question 'Where is God most likely to be found?' Hazarilalji said, 'God is wherever he's discussed' – 'bhagwan hai jaha uska charcha hai'. Let me call this form of discourse – in which I'll include the singing of raga Miyan ki Malhar – 'praise'. 'Praise' is naming, mentioning, or 'discussing', in Hazarilalji's sense. When we name or even state something, whether it's to do with a god, or an object, or a moment – if we say, 'It rains,' as Edward Thomas did in a poem – we make possible that moment or object or person. Praise presumes no prior existence – it makes present, as if for the first time, through naming. It creates, makes real. This is how Miyan ki Malhar makes the rains happen.

Govindji taught me a khayal in an afternoon raga called Gaud Sarang. It was set to rupak tala, a seven-beat (3–2–2) time signature. Hazarilalji said it was a

composition by Baiju Bawra, according to legend a contemporary and rival of Tansen's in the sixteenth century.
Here are the words:

> Mahadeva Shiva Shankare
> jatajuta trayi nayna
> neelkanthe
>
> baghambar
> trishul khappar
> gare naga
> singhi bal
> tilak biraje

Or:

> Mahadeva, Shiva, Shankar
> matted-haired three-eyed
> blue-throated one
>
> Tiger-skin-seated
> clutching trident and bowl
> neck snake-encircled
> lion-maned
> the sacred mark resting on the forehead

I was struck by the words – in enumerating his features,
they made a powerful case for Shiva. They did so not

through proselytising, but by naming the god and his accoutrements: the lyric is a cluster of nouns, beginning with three of Shiva's many names. In my translation, I've had to turn nouns like 'neelkanthe' (literally, 'blue-throated') into adjective and noun – 'blue-throated one' – for the line to make sense in English; and to add verbs – 'clutching trident and bowl' – where only nouns are mentioned: 'trishul khappar'. The syntax of Avadhi poetry makes such immediacy possible. As a result, there's less of a sense of a pre-existing object being reported after the fact; instead, there's a bringing into being, so that Shiva springs to life for the duration of the composition in the manner Hazarilalji had described ('God is wherever he's discussed'). Barthes, in his essay 'The Death of the Author', says that 'for Mallarmé . . . it is language that speaks, not the author: to write is to reach, through a pre-existing impersonality . . . that point where language alone acts, "performs", and not "oneself"'. So too, I think, with the words of the khayal in Gaud Sarang – it's language that performs; language is inseparable from Shiva's coming into existence. Comparably, the Malhars create rain.

But if there are any ragas that *do* have a mimetic quality, it's the ragas of the rainy season. There's a portentousness to the treatment of the lower octave; an emphasis on bent notes; a predominance of gamaks, tonal undulations – as if all these echoed the monsoon's upheaval.

Tansen, among the many known and unknown composers of Indian classical music, had a shrewd, poetic grasp of mimesis. For instance, his singularly named Darbari – 'of the darbar' – composed for Emperor Akbar, is his modulation on raga Asavari, which is akin to the Aeolian mode (a seven-note scale with a flat third, sixth, and seventh), where he places a subtle weight and responsibility on the flat third to suggest courtly grandeur. In Miyan ki Malhar, the raga I used to sing with my tanpura to make it rain (it was attributed to Tansen but created, actually, in the nineteenth century), the powers of evocation are even more evident. The interpreter, in this raga, must dwell for some time on the lower octave, especially on the three notes leading to the tonic, sa. The three notes are the natural sixth (dha), and the flat and natural seventh (ni): chromatic notes, in other words – immediate neighbours – which, even if they aren't sung chromatically in succession, induce a kind of foundering and dizziness. Again, in the middle octave, Tansen makes us return

to the <u>ni</u> dha ni **sa**, the cluster of chromatic notes climbing to the upper tonic, from a variety of perspectives.
You soar towards the flat seventh, fall back to the sixth,
then rise to the natural seventh, fall back, then rise. As a
consequence, the entirety of the raga becomes a sort of
leading note straining to find (while of course delaying)
a finishing-point, as with the mood preceding a thunder
shower. In a way very different, then, from the storm in
the 'Pastoral', Miyan ki Malhar explores the anticipatory
atmosphere of the rainy season, in which thunder, light-
ning, and breeze all express the desire for rainfall.

One should keep in mind Tansen's approximate dates:
1506–1589. So he's a contemporary of the European
Renaissance, which granted increasing centrality to
the human being and self-expression. Titian is at work;
Rembrandt is still to be born. In music, the romanticism
that will lead to the mimetic interpretation of notes and
their psychology – happy; sad; terrifying; soothing – is
three centuries away. Tansen is an anomaly in two traditions: in the history of the music of the world, and of
Indian music, demonstrating – through Darbari's grandeur – a deep, original feeling for representation well
before this finds its full aesthetic formulation in Europe,
and running counter, in this instance, to Hindustani classical music's non-representational tendencies.

I should make a distinction, though, between Miya
ki Malhar's representation of the rains and the sort of

116

mimesis of nature that's achieved through emotive associations to do with musical modes, shifts, and pauses in works like the 'Pastoral' or *Flight of the Bumblebee*. Firstly, its creator isn't building a world, or reproducing it, as Beethoven did in his Sixth Symphony. He's not an author; he's an interpreter. Singers of Indian classical music express their creativity by interpreting a raga; but so do composers. 'Miyan ki Malhar' means 'Miyan Tansen's version of Malhar' – what Tansen gives us is not an account of the rains, but a fresh look at something that already exists: raga Malhar, and its relationship to the rainy season. The composer is an inheritor of material he plays with, refashions, and encourages us to reconsider.

The other difference is that man isn't at the centre of Tansen's universe, whether we're referring to the historical Miyan Tansen who composed Darbari, or the creators who took on his honorific when making Miyan ki Malhar and Miyan ki Todi. With Miyan ki Malhar, we aren't viewing the rains as we would if we were looking at a painting. As David Hockney points out about a photograph-like reproduction of a canal by Canaletto, a painting, after the Renaissance, becomes a window before which we can stand and study a scene that moves, via a single perspective, to a vanishing-point. We needn't enter the scene; we're situated outside it. We own the view. The same could be said of the ingenious *Flight of the Bumblebee*, and the vantage-point it gives the audience. In Miyan ki Malhar, there's no privileged perspective vis-à-vis the shower; we submit, instead, to a melodic progression through which we, the Malhar family, and the season are connected.

Some ragas can wait for centuries to be sung. Ramdasi Malhar comes to mind. I heard a recording when I was eighteen or nineteen; it was by Amir Khan – a private, not a studio, recording, punctuated, as might be expected, by the audience's responses. It became the Amir Khan recording I loved most; Ramdasi Malhar became a favourite raga. I had never heard of it; even today, it's obscure. Two recordings by Amir Khan are in circulation on the net; both are beautiful, and neither is a studio recording. The bandish (composition) might be Amir Khan's own: 'chhaye badara kare kare' – 'black, black clouds gather'. Note that the line in English, because of the associations of the language, carries a foreboding that isn't there in Avadhi, where the same words are lit with yearning, even excitement. This is borne out by the next lines: 'umad ghumad ghana barasata garajata / tyaso hi jiyara umango hi jaye' – 'it rains densely and thunders, umad ghumad, / in just such a way my heart leaps up'. The raga has had a few other distinguished exponents (their versions mostly available as private recordings uploaded on YouTube) – Ali Akbar Khan; Bhimsen Joshi; Nazakat and Salamat Ali Khan – but I'd hazard that, despite its cultivation by a minority of practitioners, it was Amir

Khan who single-handedly brought Ramdasi Malhar to our attention.

'Ramdasi Malhar' means 'Ramdas's Malhar'. Some accounts suggest that Ramdas was a singer in Akbar's court. That would place him in the sixteenth century and make him a contemporary of Tansen's. But we can't be sure if Ramdas existed and created this version of Malhar four hundred years ago. All we have is a raga – barely, through a few recordings – which sounds, in the way Amir Khan sings it, a bit like Tansen's Miyan ki Malhar, except for its surprising juxtaposition of both the flat and the normal third, or ga.

Miyan ki Malhar lingers in the lower octave, under the surface of the sa, plumbing the lower sixth and the flat and natural seventh. Then it ascends to daylight, moving to re, the second, then to the fourth, and back again. Remember that the fourth is like a new tonic; in the blues, boogie-woogie, and rock-and-roll scale, the pentatonic is played once from the tonic and once from the fourth. Miyan ki Malhar goes up to the fourth, embraces its sense of inauguration, moves up to the fifth, pa, drops down to the pensive flat third, then rises again to the fifth, and from there proceeds to its reluctant ascent to the firmament of the upper **sa**, with the black clouds gathering in the permutations of <u>ni</u> dha ni **sa**. Reaching the upper tonic, it collapses back to the lower tonic, with this phrase marking the swift descent:

sa <u>ni</u> pa <u>ga</u>, ma re sa

Ramdasi Malhar unfolds very similarly, without making too much of a fuss over the sixth and sevenths in the lower octave, but as it climbs it touches the natural third – a note absent from Miyan ki Malhar – and then, on touching the upper sa, it descends, in Amir Khan's renditions, in a phrase identical to the one above, except that it will incorporate, again, the natural third as the notes fall back:

sa <u>ni</u> pa ga ma re, pa <u>ga</u> ma re sa

To listen to Hindustani classical music is to enter a universe centred on certain metamorphoses, including proximate notes changing from one to the other. Ga to <u>ga</u> has great meaning in this universe. The natural third has a buoyancy that corresponds to the renewal the rains offer: the washed leaves and air; the burgeoning of, and movement in, the environment. The flat third, following immediately, introduces reflectiveness – also in keeping with the dark days of Sravan, from mid-July to mid-August. All we know of Ramdas is this: that the rains brought his sensibility to life at one moment, as the tender caressing of the natural ga on the way up and the unexpected drop to it on the journey down indicate: and, at the next moment, with the flat third, they made him reflective, and look inward. He was seized, in consecutive instants, by divergent moods. We know nothing else about Ramdas. The boundary between knowing and not knowing him is negligible but real, like the boundary separating the flat ga from the natural, or the demarcation between melancholy and anticipation.

For more than four centuries, this raga waited for Ustad Amir Khan's arrival. Following the raga finding the right singer comes its belated entry into the world.

Occasionally, when there's a squall, or a series of thunder showers at the wrong time of the year, you wonder for a second what will happen to Kalidasa and the *Meghaduta*, to the Malhars and the ragas of the seasons.

Ragas have a degree of translatability. They can be exported to a different climate and soundscape, and judged on innate musical beauty. But since ragas belong to a milieu where every sound, and not just the notes of the raga, finds a place in the text – including the sound of a ceiling fan – it also, to a significant extent, resists travel: this is undeniable, at least to the Indian ear, which, without realising it, is accustomed to multiple, conflicting dimensions of sound. The raga can inhabit silence no more than the Indian ear can.

The question is whether the raga can be exported to a future in which the sounds and effects we're familiar with, and which are often generated by the weather, no longer exist. Whatever the changes in history and geography in the last two thousand years – empires emerging and falling; rivers drying up – whatever the 'inseparable gulf', as Tagore put it, between our time and Kalidasa's, natives of this land, as well as the raga, have been living, weather-wise, in the same continuum for millennia.

Kalidasa's sravan is Tagore's, as it is ours: one of the features of an intangible, ever-changing inheritance. Could a Malhar be extrapolated to a future when the monsoon is no longer what we know it to be?

When I wasn't practising classical music, I was listening to it. My preference was the voice: not only because it's said to be the basis of Indian music, with instruments taking their cue from vocal modulation, but because, to me, it's the most sensuous vehicle melody has.

Not everything I listened to was khayal: any form that embraced the raga interested me. So I listened repeatedly to K. L. Saigal and Mehdi Hassan: two singers, generations apart – from India and Pakistan respectively (though Mehdi Hassan was born in Jaipur) – who gave, via the raga, the ghazal its fullest twentieth-century expression. I listened to the greatest popular singer in Bengal, S. D. Burman; to his *ragpradhan* or 'raga-predominant' songs in particular. By the seventies, his achievement in the popular Bengali song was as good as forgotten, and he was famous as a composer for Hindi movies. I got to hear his songs because one of my maternal uncles was a fanatical devotee, and a wonderful singer in S. D. Burman's style. I listened to Pannalal Bhattacharya's *shyamasangeet*: songs to Kali. I noted the delicacy and the affection with which he sang of the Mother's eccentricities. I puzzled over his suicide, but there was no key to it in his music.

*

Govindji told me, earnestly, that one should keep the best company and, similarly, listen only to the best music. I didn't know about company; at the age of eighteen, I'd taken a decision not to have much to do with people who didn't interest me.

In music, too, I didn't listen to anything I didn't find beautiful. I discovered that, although there was a paucity of people I was left with after my decision, there was a large remainder where music was concerned. One didn't *have* to listen to the second-rate, let alone the bad. There was an abundance of the enthralling: Nazakat and Salamat Ali Khan; Kishori Amonkar; Veena Sahasrabuddhe; Rasoolan Bai; Jasraj; D. V. Paluskar; Bhimsen Joshi; Jagdish Prasad; Vismadev Chatterjee; Kumar Gandharva; Abdul Karim Khan; A. Kanan; Kesarbai Kerkar; Barkat Ali Khan; Bade Ghulam Ali Khan; Mogubai Kurdikar; Sharafat Hussein Khan – to name just classical vocalists.

I love listening to the world. Music is only one of the many sounds available to the ear.

It took travel to bring this awareness. I didn't know till I started living in London how much I'd missed sounds when growing up on the twelfth storey in Malabar Hill, and on the twenty-fifth storey later.

What does listening involve? For one, it has congruences with looking. The eye is an opening in the body through which the consciousness receives images, and through which it also repeatedly steps out. The eye might passively register a monument or traffic light. But when you stand on a balcony, or enter a lane by mistake, your eye lets the self leak out and be possessed by the lane's life, and, through desire, become part of its existence, forgetting your own. Similarly, you look again, from the balcony, at a house you've never visited, and you're seized by a reverie. Looking, at this point, isn't taking in. It's losing yourself.

The ear, too, is an opening. To listen might mean to passively take in: an instruction, or a communication. Or the ear may be enveloped, as when you're listening to music. Or listening could involve desire, on hearing, for instance, a sound from a neighbouring house. You don't know the source of the sound. Involuntarily, you depart yourself and travel towards it. You're gripped by a yearning for – and, through yearning, a slipping into – the unseen.

This is characteristic of everyday experiences in India; again and again, you feel the impact of the invisible. A mynah on a neighbouring verandah; the scraping of pigeons' claws on the air conditioner; music practice; bursts of hammering; women talking – all these comprise the invisible. Listening becomes indistinguishable from longing.

The artist to first capture this in the context of India was Jean Renoir. I have in mind *The River*, a minor work in his oeuvre, except for its soundtrack. A story, based on Rumer Godden's novel, unfolds on the screen, about an expatriate family in a riverine Indian town. In every frame, presences – that have no immediate bearing on the characters we're watching – are introduced to us through the soundtrack. We watch the film; we pursue the slender narrative – but, through listening, we frequently sense possibilities, and an elsewhere, that the visuals won't disclose. We're touched by the invisible, and we respond by stepping out of ourselves. Much of our attention is on the story; but not, because of the soundtrack, all of it.

Renoir visited India in 1951 to make this film, and he was shown around by a filmmaker *manqué* and Renoir enthusiast, Satyajit Ray, who'd complete his own *Pather*

Panchali four years later. The most important thing that Ray learnt from Renoir was not in the realm of image, but of sound. It was probably a lesson passed on from one subconscious to another, because Renoir's achievement in *The River* and Ray's debt to it were never discussed. But almost every frame in Ray is qualified and formed by the invisible. This is because Ray's soundtracks are notable not only for his music; through the leakage into the ear, they're almost always absent-minded, elsewhere, and not fully present. The eye watching a Ray film looks on in absorption; the ear is picking up sounds not only to do with what's being looked at, but what's on the edge of the visual. A delay between looking and listening occurs in the frame.

Ray calls this delay 'poetry'. He describes it in relation to another filmmaker he admired, John Ford:

Much of the best things in a Ford film has the mysterious, indefinable quality of poetry. Because some of them appear casual – even accidental – it is difficult to realise how much experience and mastery lie behind them. Let me describe one such moment from the film *Fort Apache*. Two men stand talking on the edge of a deep ravine. There is a broken bottle lying alongside. One man gives it a casual kick and sends it flying over the edge. A few seconds later, in a gap in the conversation, the sound track registers the faintest of clinks. That's all.

Two things are striking: the moment in the film, and what Ray notices. Audiences attend to conversations between characters and not necessarily the silences in between; but the 'gap' that follows the conversation is not straightforward silence – it carries a potential hinted at by the 'clink'. In other words, we're supposed to read the soundtrack not in relation to the story, but as we would a piece of music. The 'clink' awakens our dormant sense of the unseen: not a task usually associated with cinema, a visual medium, but one that's important to the sort of artist Ray is. Ray, of course, was a committed, avowed listener of Western classical music. But a different sort of training is at work here – to do with living in Calcutta; being drawn to noises whose origins aren't clear; with realising there are no reliable characteristics marking out silence as being distinct from sound.

In North Indian poetry, the breeze is a metaphor for listening. This has been true from classical poetry and Kalidasa onwards. For Kalidasa, the breeze in the *Meghaduta* ('The Cloud-Messenger') does what sound does in a Ray soundtrack: signalling to the unseen, it might come in through an opening, maybe a window; the window itself is a metaphor for openings in our body, most commonly the eye, but, in India, more persuasively for the ear. In the *Meghaduta*, the breeze gives the Yaksha an immediate inkling of the beloved he can neither see nor possess: 'The breezes from the snowy peaks have just burst upon the leaf-buds of deodar trees and, redolent of their oozing resin, blow southward. I embrace those breezes, fondly imagining they have lately touched your form, O perfect one!' For me, this intimation of the invisible also works as an account of listening.

In Hindi films from the fifties to the late sixties, when the songs in those films and the way they were shot were at their most luminous, there's a frequent convergence between the action of the breeze – that is, the play of the invisible, whose effects can only be judged by, say, the movements of strands of hair on the forehead – and the singing of the song. There's a close-up shot of the actress's face; a breeze is blowing; she's singing. Some songs are themselves about a breeze:

> thandi hawaen leherake aayen
> rut bhi jwaan tumko yahan kaise bulaye

> The cool breeze comes in waves.
> The season's young:
> how do I call you here?

This is a replay of the Yaksha's desire, and of the breeze's implicit connection, through word and music, to listening – that is, to what can't be seen.

Inasmuch as there's no pure silence, inasmuch as sound is random and recurring, listening can happen at any time.

The notion of music as a separate representational 'composition' about our emotions, or the concert hall as a designated space for performance, dulls our vulnerability to sound. When we hear a sound, we create it even before we've identified it: *we* make it a sound as much as whoever it is that's produced it. Listening, then, involves not just focusing, as at a concert; it's a state of distraction.

John Cage was a critic of the post-Enlightenment idea of the concert space and the representational musical composition: from this comes his work *4'33"*, wrongly – as he pointed out – thought to be four minutes and thirty-three seconds of silence. The performers put down their instruments – the one thing that distinguishes them from the audience, or the 'listeners'. Everybody listens, also picking up the sounds the others make; everyone, while breathing, makes some sound.

In my parents' record collection was a long-playing album of Amar Pal's folk songs. These songs were mainly bhatiali (attributed to East Bengali boatmen) and baul (a Vaishnav or Krishna-worshipping sect, whose name means 'crazed'). I admired Pal's calm; the way he didn't let spiritual fervour make pitch secondary.

Two songs I remember for their glowing litany of morning sounds:

> Rai jago Rai jago jago
> shuk o shari bale

Or:

> Rai, wake up, Rai, wake up,
> cry the shuk and shari birds.

Another song began:

> Jai Radhe Jai Radhe Gobinda
> Jai Radhe Jai Radhe
> bhor samay kale kokila dake dale
> bhramara Hari guna gaye re

Or:

> Jai Radhe Jai Radhe Gobinda
> Jai Radhe Jai Radhe
> cries the cuckoo on the branch at dawn
> the bees sing Hari's praises

The effect of these early recordings derives from Pal rendering the songs with pitch-perfect undramatic precision – the musical equivalent of matter-of-factness – as if the words said nothing extraordinary. The mythical shuk and shari birds are exhorting Radha to wake; the kokil (or cuckoo) is singing Jai Radhe; the bees are praising Hari. This, according to the Baul, is what we wake up to each day. The phrase 'Hari guna' means 'the virtues of Hari', and 'guna gaye' is 'to sing the praises of'. But the word 'gungun' in Bengali means 'humming', and it's ascribed to bees. Through a pun, the bees' hum is con-flated with their paeans to Krishna. Waking, then, is an occasion to listen to the world busily acknowledging its divine provenance. My entry into the day was differ-ent. But the words made me think of small towns in Bengal where I'd gone to visit relatives – so remote from Bombay – and holidays in my uncle's house in south Calcutta. Bird cry, insect hum, even domestic sound became more real there. I learnt how sound – divorced from word, divorced even from what we commonly take to be a musical note – is often 'saying' something.

Besides the flute-music of the cowherd Krishna, there's another bit of sound in the stories related to him. It's to do with the anklets, or the payal, that Radha wears, whose vibrations risk waking up the husband's family as she goes out to see her lover. Anyone who's familiar with thumri, bhajan, and even khayal will know the sounds these bells make and the terror that accompanies them. Here are the first two lines of a khayal in raga Nand:

> payal mori baje jhananananana
> ati dar lage piya

Or:

> My payal goes jhananananana.
> I feel so afraid, love.

We're Radha now; our aim is to be not found out. We're in suspenseful abeyance. Jagdish Prasad sings a thumri in raga Khamaj:

> tose nahi bolu re
> balam chhed mat ja

> sej chadhat mori payal baje
> jage saans nanadiya
> sainya jiya na jala

Or:

> I won't speak to you
> if you tease me, love
>
> As I climb on the bed my payal rings out.
> Mother-in-law and sister-in-law stir!
> Dearest, don't drive me mad.

Who would have thought that this sound could imply transgression? In these songs, it alerts us to the passage between worlds, one social, the other unfamiliar.

To listen is to be distracted. It might lead to the slowing down of a task at hand. This is the effect that Hindustani classical music, when it's overheard, induces: an enthralment accompanied by an inattention to other things.

In the word 'maya' lies the key to our relationship to the raga; but 'maya' isn't easy to translate. It's a Sanskrit word; the meanings that were given to it by the Sanskritist Monier Monier-Williams (1819–99) – 'illusion, unreality' – have held sway in the Anglophone world. According to this interpretation, Hindus believe that the visible world is 'illusion'. 'Maya' is described as a 'jaal' or 'web' – the 'web' of 'unreality' we're all enmeshed in, and confuse for the real. It's a notion echoed by the Christian idea of 'vanity': 'vanity of vanities; all is vanity', in Ecclesiastes. I too grew up thinking 'maya', for the Hindus, was 'illusion' – according to this theory, the furniture in my house, the people I knew, including my parents, weren't 'real' – and, since this isn't a thought you can live with, I let it be. From Bengali speech, however – especially the speech of the people who worked part-time in my uncle's house in Calcutta – I got another sense of the word: 'attachment', 'affectionate attachment', even 'love'. Not necessarily romantic love; just a pull towards someone or something. Other possible words for it are 'spell' and 'enchantment'; but they should suggest temporality. Maya lasts a limited period. The limited period could be a lifetime, or an afternoon. But it entails slowing down. On my last afternoon in Calcutta in my uncle's house, I would stand on the terrace, unable, in my heart, to be part of anything, and the maidservant would make it worse by smiling sadly: 'This time tomorrow you won't be here!' I would be in Bombay! Maya is characterised by ennui and inaction. Ennui has a relation to enchantment, to becoming enthralled by the beautiful.

When you listen to Hindustani classical music, you're gripped by maya. This is especially true during the alaap, when the exposition – the tabla playing at a slowed-down tempo – takes place in free time. The listener is enmeshed in the note's pupal emergence, its relationship to already-explored notes and the notes to come. They're aware of the web's beauty and fragility. They may not be seated, in a posture of attention; they may be on the floor, leaning to one side, or semi-upright. Small things make them gasp: the má in Yaman, refusing to meet the fifth; the descent from pa to re in Chhaya Nat; the wave rising from the má to dhaivat and then falling back to ma natural in Kedar; the ni in Khamaj's descent. When moved by a phrase, they'll neither keep their head still nor nod in agreement; they'll shake it from side to side. The gesture covers a range of emotions: surprise, delight, resignation.

At certain phrases, the listener sighs 'Ah!' or 'Aha!' This means wonder and pity – wonder at beauty; pity for the pain that creates beauty.

When Hindi films entered a period of unprecedented musical innovation, from the late fifties to the early seventies, extending from the black-and-white era into colour, a new cinematic idiom was created for those three or four minutes of song during which the actors would lip-sync to the voices of the great 'playback' singers. It was called 'song picturisation'; or just 'picturisation'. It comprised a break in narrative, plot, and drama; 'picturisation' enshrined the superfluity of song. 'Why must Hindi films have songs at every opportunity?' was the rationalist refrain I grew up with. By the time I was seventeen or eighteen, I'd discovered 'picturisation', which, at its best, recognises that the plot must be put on hold as music introduces us to a reality that's of a different order from the rest of the film.

Picturisation was not just to do with singing. It's to do with listening, and attention. Unlike the Hollywood musical, which takes its cue from Broadway and emphasises movement and choreography, the three or four minutes of picturisation frequently underline stillness: the radiant, sometimes backlit, face of the one singing; and, like a mirror-image, the face of the listener. Again, in contrast to Hollywood, the actors' bodies are secondary; instead, the faces are studies in ecstasy and bewilderment.

140

One of the most acute depictions of how we both make and listen to music occurs in the 1965 film *Hum Dono* ('Us Two'). The name itself is a pun – on the relationship between man and woman, lover and beloved, self and consciousness. ('There are two birds, two sweet friends, who dwell on the self-same branch,' says the *Mundaka Upanishad*. 'The one eats the fruit thereof, and the other looks on in silence.')

The film is about two men who are in the army and have to go to war, leaving their fiancées behind. They become friends. Little fuss is overtly made of the fact that, despite one having a moustache and the other being clean-shaven, they're identical to each other. Both men are played by Dev Anand.

One evening, they sit, drinking, and talking about how hard it is not to think of loved ones. One of them, bending over his glass, begins to sing a ghazal:

> kabhi khud pe kabhi halat pe rona aya
> baat niklegi to har baat pe rona aya

Roughly:

> Sometimes it was myself, sometimes the state of
>   things that made me cry.
> Once the subject came up, every subject made
>   me cry.

The other does a double take; then a look of empathy and immersion comes to his face as the song goes on:

> I'd convinced myself I'd forgotten her.
> What's happened today; what is it that makes me cry?

With the next verse, the friend looks at the singer strangely, then surrenders to the mood:

> For what reason do we live, and whom do we live for?
> Time and time again these questions made me cry.

The singer gets up; the friend puts an arm around his shoulder. They walk out, backs to the camera:

> We don't cry from pitying another, O friend.
> It's some thought about ourselves that makes us cry.

What's striking about the images is how the person singing is also the one who's listening. They have different identities, different ranks in the army; but they're also one person. The listener delights inexplicably, even though what they're hearing is born of pain; you see this in Dev Anand's indecipherable expressions. Dev Anand the singer is almost unaware of his double's proximity; alone in vocalising sorrow, he's in a state of quasi-innocence. Our eyes move from singer's face to listener's. The person who delights and the person who suffers are one.

Govindji went with us to Calcutta on one of our visits, to sing at a concert. He stayed in our flat in Sunny Park. I practised with him.

This was an opportunity to buy a tanpura for myself. The best musical instruments were said to come from Calcutta – for the quality of the craftsmanship and of the materials. The gourd from which the urns or tumbas of the tanpura and sitar were made grew locally.

We went to Rashbehari Avenue, to Hemen and Company. Hemen was there. He rebuffed us: no tanpuras were available. We stepped back on to the pavement, trying to conjure up plan B. Then we were summoned back. Someone in the shop – the sarod player, Dhyanesh Khan, Ustad Ali Akbar Khan's son – had recognised my guru. Govindji taught his mother, who lived in Cuffe Parade in Bombay: she was one of Ali Akbar Khan's four wives. Dhyanesh had said something to the implacable Hemen. As a result, I bought, for nine hundred rupees, a tanpura he'd been making for Ali Akbar Khan.

The tanpura has four strings. These are played repeatedly. The tanpura is a drone – an ill-fitting term for such a significant instrument. Its outer string is tuned to the fifth, but, if there's no fifth in the raga, it's tuned to the

143

natural seventh. If the raga's dominant interval is the fourth, or ma, then that's the note the outer string is tuned to.

The two strings in the middle form a pair. They're tuned to the tonic. The string that's played last is thicker, and tuned to the tonic or sa of the lower octave. Two notes – that is, the tonic in the middle and lower octaves, and the fifth, or seventh, or fourth, depending on the raga – create the architecture the raga inhabits. This is not a solid structure; it's a form of maya, a web, a resonance rather than two separate standalone notes.

What engenders the weave? A few things. The first comes from the strings limiting themselves to two notes. These represent a primary musical relationship, and establish a vastness that multiple notes can't. Then there's the repetition. Anything – names; words; notes – repeated infinitely loses meaning. Repetition takes sa and pa out of the bounds of their recognised roles. The tanpura may be the cultural forefather of trance music. 'Trance' itself is an offshoot of maya.

An astonishing technological innovation contributes to the strings' web-like effect. It involves slipping a tiny bow of thread under the strings, where they rest on the bridge at the tanpura's base. You move the thread up and down till you hit the spot that produces a fuzziness, an impurity. A 'clean' tone is anathema to tanpura and sitar. The fuzz imparted via overdrive to the electric guitar in the sixties was always fundamental to the tanpura. It allowed the remnant of one note to resonate into another.

When I learnt how to tune and play the tanpura – even striking the four strings with your index and middle fingers has to be learnt – I was told by my guru, 'Don't keep time with the tanpura. It isn't meant for keeping time.' When you play a string instrument as you sing, there's an instinctual human tendency to maintain a rhythm. With the tanpura, you pluck the strings consecutively at a tempo of your choosing – usually a medium one – and perform this action repeatedly. But the speed at which you play the strings is unrelated to the tempo at which you're singing.

This studied lack of correlation – between the tanpura's rhythm and the song's – a correlation that, in most musical circumstances, would be normal, is one of the many small but crucial insights of which the Hindustani classical tradition is constituted. It frees things up by rethinking the framework.

To suddenly not know what to do next, to be at a loose end just before going somewhere, is to be listening. To be lost – to pause and retrace your steps – is also to listen.

I find this retracing is not only the way I attend to Indian classical music, but also to Joni Mitchell. If I stand up to turn on Bluetooth, and then begin playing 'Rainy Night House', or 'The Gallery', or 'Both Sides Now', I start walking in a small orbit as the opening bars are played on the piano, or the chords struck, reluctant to stray too far from the speaker. Either I'm lost, or I have to go somewhere and don't want to.

I went to London as a student in 1983. My understanding of life changed soon after.

First, I noticed the silence: the closed windows, and the interiority of experience. Growing up in Bombay, this kind of enclosedness – even on the twelfth or twenty-fifth storey – wouldn't have struck me as plausible. Here, it was a fact.

Then there was the significance attributed to noise: the noise that others made; the noise I made. Sound seemed to be culturally and racially charged; it tended to have an alienness to it, to comprise an incursion. I began to suffer from the sounds others made. I began to inflict my sound on others. Silence too was cultural: it was the proper context for thought and civility.

I'd said goodbye to my acoustic guitar in 1982. Until then, I'd continued to sing and write songs while doing my riyaaz and making slow progress as a classical musician. By the end of 1982, I withdrew from the world as a singer-songwriter, as other singer-songwriters evidently had: Neil Young, Joni Mitchell.

My guru helped me buy a second tanpura. The one from Hemen was far too big to carry abroad. It would have to stay at home. Where home was had become moot – my father's days in the company were ending, as was our time on the twenty-fifth storey. Govindji took me to a man called Ambalal Sitari. As his name suggests, he was a musician and a maker of musical instruments. He lived in a building on Breach Candy. Govindji told me he'd fashioned something new: a portable tanpura. The bespoke one Mr Sitari would make for me was, if I remember right, going to be the second of the species. When the object was ready, its size seemed perfect: like a ukulele's or banjo's. The sound was less persuasive; the strings wouldn't really buzz, however much you adjusted the position of the threads looped at the bottom. I took it to London.

I became guarded in London when it came to music. Ten days after my arrival, I was sitting with my parents and my uncle in an Indian restaurant in Belsize Village. We'd ordered dinner. My parents and uncle talked; I hummed to myself. I wasn't aware I was humming. Contrary to Descartes, awareness of oneself seldom comes from within: it comes from others. I was unmindful of the fact that I sang well outside the demarcated hours of practice, partly to hone a phrase, partly in a mood of discovery or engrossment. Self-consciousness came when I realised that a young man at another table was mimicking me. He was parodying my glissandos; they probably sounded strange to him. There were three at his table: he, another man, and a young woman. She shushed him

148

discreetly. I was mortified – mainly because I was audible. In India, the subconscious floats on the unbroken auditory buzz of the environment while the conscious mind focuses or daydreams. A week before term, I was now – at least where music was concerned – plunged into an unobtrusive scrutiny.

I saw that people hardly spoke to each other on the Tube, although they did make eye contact through the reflections on the glass. If a group of people spoke loudly, they were invariably men, and supporters of a football team. You avoided meeting their eye. If a group of white people happened to be conversing loudly and unmenacingly, you found, as you went closer, that they were Italian.

Mostly, English commuters exuded what Nietzsche called 'ironical self-consciousness' – a keen sense of the self, and of its separateness. It entailed a preternaturally sensitive mode of interaction, involving hearing more than sight – that is, constantly expecting the other to speak or make a sound – which led to a consciously heightened form of listening that, as it turned out, was contagious. I began to succumb to it myself.

I stayed for a few months in the International Students House on Great Portland Street. I didn't take a room in the University College London hall of residence primarily because I didn't want to be found out as a singer. Even before moving to England, my riyaaz, in anticipation, was freighted with added meaning. At ISH, I presumed the 'international' context would make me less noticeable.

Just how thin floors and walls are in the West was an education for me. One evening, as I was sitting in my room, I clearly heard a conversation in the next room. The wall was a formality; they may as well have been in my room. The sound troubled me deeply – I froze – mainly because I now knew that I was as audible.

I began to practise by stealth, guessing when my neighbours' rooms were empty. I did practise, though; a singer has no option. I have a memory of singing Asavari – a morning raga which my guru had taught me some months earlier – late one morning when I thought people had gone for lectures. Ambalal Sitari's tanpura lay on my lap. I felt at one remove from the bandish, not to mention the room I was in.

In two months, I moved to a studio flat on Warren Street. This stretched my father, though he never once gave an indication. But the rent rose, and I knew I must spend and eat carefully.

That year's and next year's music came to me from other people's flats and from TV. (I could live in London without friends but not without a television, so I'd got one from Radio Rentals.) Culture Club dominated; they were on TV, and 'Karma Chameleon' wafted in from everywhere. My mother, who'd stayed on for a month, studied Boy George and his cohort – we often watched TV together – not with animosity or stoicism, but with a sweet suspension of disbelief. She was listening to him, as she did to all music.

Then, like a throbbing tumour, there was 'Relax!' by Frankie Goes to Hollywood. From upstairs, where a Mauritian called Sanjay Bhuckory was studying law, came Lionel Richie's mellifluous pleading: 'Hello! Is it me you're looking for?' The question was posed over and over, indifferent to the quasi-poverty and paranoia I inhabited. Then, as I was trying to make sense of my world, my being here, came Wham!'s 'Freedom'. It's not as if there was no talent in this new world. It's just that talent was spent so lightly. Artists in 1983 seemed to treat their talent – their gift – with the casualness with which another generation had treated life, or money.

I didn't mention Duran Duran, but haven't forgotten them. What I mean is: the groundwork was laid by the music around my room for me to feel it was unnecessary for me to listen to it. I began to disengage from pop, then cut myself off from it completely. A musical system that had been peripheral to me as a boy – Hindustani classical music – became my mainstay. I spent much more time on it than I did on University College London.

I didn't have the big tanpura with me, but I'd managed to lug over a harmonium, checking it in as 'fragile'. It survived. I placed it against the wall to the left of the door to the room that served as bedroom with dining table (the kitchen and bathroom were adjoining the hallway). Here, as with children being punished in the American comic books I'd grown up with by being made to face a wall, I sat on the floor for stretches of time singing Tagore songs, bhajans, and Mehdi Hassan's ghazals. My exact position was important, because the room was a map; I knew when I was under the kitchen upstairs, or a bedroom, and located myself and my singing accordingly. I imagined the geography of the flat below. As with heat in London houses, I speculated if sound rises or falls.

I had purchased a small three-in-one, from which a turntable slipped out in cuckoo-clock fashion when you pressed a button. I had brought nine or ten records to London: Subinoy Roy magisterially singing Tagore songs; Mehdi Hassan's *Ghazals*; Pannalal's shyama sangeet, songs to Kali. The rest were singers of khayal – Bade Ghulam Ali, Kishori Amonkar, Bhimsen Joshi. There was nothing from my earlier hoard: Crosby, Stills and Nash; Janis Joplin, etc. In this way, as if on a maritime vessel, I prepared for a decades-long journey. I listened to no more pop for sixteen years. Not until, that is, I 'officially' went home in 1999. It's not uncommon to be exiled from home at home and to re-evaluate its meaning abroad. This is the path of modernity – at least Indian modernity. Michael Madhusudan Dutt, arguably Bengal's first modern poet, wanted to be an English poet and wrote poetry in English, until, in 1860, he did a volte-face and embarked on a Bengali epic, taking his subject matter from the *Ramayana* and his cue from Milton. Later, migrating to London and then Versailles, he introduced the Petrarchan sonnet to Bengali. The exile might exile themselves from exile, making of exile a homecoming. This is true of Dutt, who continued to write letters in English, but never again wrote an English poem. I, too, never sang a rock song till the end of the millennium. Granted, my 'turn' had taken place in Bombay, in 1978. But, in London, it deepened and extended its scope. Any music post-'Freedom' may as well have happened on another planet.

*

Given the creaking floorboards in 16 Warren Street, my singing reached my neighbours, and I practised those three years in a state of siege. Not that I sang loudly, like an opera singer; but the notes would have sounded weird, even to Indian-origin tenants who subsisted on rap and hip hop. When Sanjay Bhuckory finished his law degree, Gujarati Africans moved in. Below me was a woman called Debbie. They all kept hours completely at odds with mine, sleeping at 3 or 4 a.m., waking after midday. My nights – night after night – were spent in a terror of apprehension: would I be able to sleep? All hip hop meant to me was a bass thud after midnight. Nevertheless, I descended on the rug after 9.30 a.m. to practise Bhairav. I knew 9.30 a.m. was midnight for my neighbours, but there was little I could do about it. Once, I remember starting to sing Gaud Sarang after midday (even in this context, I adhered to the ragas' time-cycle) – 'Mahadev, Shiv, Shankar / matted-haired, three-eyed one' – and then hearing stirrings above, disgruntled, incoherent, each heavy footfall a protest.

I spent Christmas in the flat. There was silence in London. I staved it off with Christmas fare on TV: *Morecambe and Wise*; a luminous rerun of *Monsieur Hulot's Holiday*. My mother often called my father 'Monsieur Hulot', and I could never watch the film without thinking of this sobriquet. The dead calm of the street was broken by singing: 'Here we go, here we go, here we go,' a demoniacal tide which swelled and vanished. This was the last time I was in London over Christmas: why stay back in an abandoned city?

There was a garage near where I lived. Twice, in those three years, I heard a car horn. It confused me ontologically, like the sight of a person resembling a loved one who you know is dead.

I began to go home frequently. Just as I spent the bare minimum of time at University College London, I spent more of the year in Bombay than I did in London. I calculated that the fares on Gulf Air cost less than what I'd spend in London during the short term-end breaks in the academic year. But I wasn't going home to save money. I was going home to see my parents. I was going home to resume unconstrained riyaaz with Girdharji and Hazarilalji; to get my guru, always hard-pressed for time, to teach me new bandishes; to return the raga (this had become important to me) to the milieu it was used to.

So I never received permanent residency in the UK. That is, I made myself ineligible by becoming absent for long stretches of time. This pattern characterises the ongoing relationship I've had with Britain over thirty-six years. I've been constantly away from India because I was a student in England; later, I began to teach there; my life as a published writer began there. I'm constantly away from Britain because of variations on the emotional and spiritual demands I experienced as an undergraduate: my desire to see my parents; my wife's decision and mine to bring up our daughter in Calcutta; the practical and emotional contexts of music, to sit down with accompanists to riyaaz; the appositeness of writing at home, though I have no fixed spot where I write in my flat, and, if need be, can write – and sing – anywhere in the world.

My parents vacated the flat on the twenty-fifth storey and moved to a building in Worli called Sea Glimpse. It must have had a view of the sea when it first rose; there was none now. My father had bought the flat some years ago because he could afford the price. It had a rat problem: they scuttled democratically from floor to floor. The lift said: USE LIFT AT YOUR OWN RISK. My father could get used to anything. He saw life in distinct phases: he'd lived in Malabar Hill, then Cuffe Parade; he would now live here. My mother, temperamentally his opposite, could get used to anything he was used to. Staying with them on my first visit, I suggested to my father that he sell this place and look for something further afield; maybe Bandra, which, an hour's drive from the city proper, might offer a better property at a lower price.

My parents sold the Worli flat and acquired a small one in a lane called St Cyril Road. I kept abreast of the negotiations, the last-minute panics, on the phone. My mother parted with jewellery, and my father borrowed some money from the bank. I entered the new flat around midnight after returning to Bombay in December.

*

My mother and I talked into the night: about London; post-retirement life; Bandra. Then I went to bed. I should have slept late, but was startled awake by a horrific cacophony. It took my sentient mind three or four seconds to conclude: this must be birdcall. I had nothing to compare it to. I'd grown up in flats too high up, or in homes that weren't surrounded by enough trees to support this volume of bird-life. I grasped what the noise was through rapid elimination.

The flat was on the third storey. My parents' bedroom and mine shared a balcony. Opposite us was a three-storeyed house; not a new building like ours. A man who wore thick glasses, probably in his seventies, sat on the balcony for long periods, directly at eye level. Sometimes a woman in a dress joined him. I thought they might be Parsi. They'd sit together, the man turned to the right, the woman facing St Cyril Road, neither unaware, nor taking cognisance, of the other. Twice, I saw the woman let loose a torrent of words at the man in a powerful voice. The man responded by not responding, by keeping vigil as she reprimanded him. I began to acknowledge to myself how much I loved this view in comparison to the sea I'd grown up looking out on.

I began to find out what it meant to live on the third storey. It was to be an insect who sees indistinctly and is wrapped, concealed, by an excess of sound. This was in contrast to my angelic suspension on the twelfth storey;

my flailing about in mid-air on the twenty-fifth. Most of all, it was in contrast to the stillness I'd found in houses and streets in London, a quiet which grew unbearable on Sundays.

Govindji was a bit disappointed by the proportions of the flat, which was small, especially in comparison to the earlier apartments. But he inspected it and rallied, won over by its charm.

Practice sessions with Govindji, Girdharji on the tabla, and sometimes with Hazarilalji either on the tabla or harmonium, took place in the sitting room, or in my bedroom, or in my parents' room. Wherever we sat, there was access, through the open doors of two balconies, to St Cyril Road. Besides the cries of schoolchildren and the revving of autorickshaws, there were sounds peculiar to the area. A high-pitched bell was struck late in the afternoon: although I never saw him, I learnt it was the kulfiwala announcing his entrance.

Hearing the bell, Girdharji said: 'Pancham me bol raha hai'; or, 'It's hit the fifth!' That is, the fifth, or pa in relation to my tonic – probably F on the harmonium – to which he would have tuned the tabla with a hammer a little while ago. It wasn't a comment he'd have made in Cuffe Parade. Since Indian music has no natural C to which the scales are tied via the piano, the tonic and its intervals are potentially everywhere in your proximity. The Indian classical musician is a comparativist; not only does he test notes in relation to each other in a

raga, he hears extensions of that relationship in his surroundings. There may be conflicts too; the ear of the
classical musician is subconsciously alert to air condi-
tioning because a drop in temperature can affect the tanpura's tuning, but also because the air conditioner may
be humming at a pitch, a note, that's absent in the raga.
Girdharji's remark makes me think of Bharata's analo-
gies attributing the origins of the seven notes of the scale
to animal and bird sounds. He may have included indus-
trial sounds if he'd lived in the twentieth century.

Bandra was predominantly a Roman Catholic area.
This gave it its unhomelikeness. St Andrew's church
and school were a few minutes' walk away from my
parents. The area had its own economy; even its own
food, vendors, and vagrants. A young Maharashtrian
came regularly to my mother with a basket of produce.
A man on a bicycle cart supplied bread in the afternoon.
It was wrapped in paper and slipped in through a gap in
the doorway, to my mother, or me, or a maid. Touching
it, I'd find it was warm. It was like a still-living thing,
one of the many beings that enter the universe for a
short period and disappear before they become old or
unwanted. I touched it a couple of times: the warmth
was like a sting – I must have had something of the
damp of London in me, because I'd begun to associate
warmth with life.

*

The third-storey flat placed my consciousness in the world, near the street. St Cyril Road became part of my education as a writer and musician. The open window in my room confirmed to me that the self has no centre; it's never fully present; it's always overhearing something. Warren Street was an education too. It represented interiority. It made me realise the pervasiveness of psychology, inwardness, and silence. Writing and music must be a liberation from these, just as St Cyril Road was an escape from Warren Street.

Of the three – Govindji, his younger brother Girdharji, and his brother-in-law Hazarilalji – it was Hazarilalji who loved me most openly. He was lucky; often people don't express love because of some constraint they can do nothing about, but Hazarilalji, whatever his failings – I was once told he got drunk every night; Govindji was cold with him because he thought he scrounged off him – was unfettered in his generosity. I learnt a lot from him, though he was never acknowledged – by me or others – as my 'guru'. This wasn't a withholding; it was the way things became. Govindji gave me a model of delicacy, of how to aim to sing difficult phrases with casualness. Hazarilalji held my hand. He presented me with his more ordinary, faltering, increasingly rusty vocal abilities, and helped me get my work done.

He was a short man. I don't know how aware he was of this. He once told me that human beings had once been giants and that their stature had decreased the more corrupt they became. We were both convinced we were living in a dreadful era.

He was a kathak dancer. He told me he'd been a dancer in Maharaja Man Singh's court in Jaipur. An accident in his youth aborted his career, and he became a dance teacher. He was largely unlettered, but had an imperious refinement in his understanding of music, dance, and poetry. As a person, he was intransigent, difficult, easy, paternal, needy. He was lazy and painstaking. I got to know the rudiments of kathak dance keeping his company – not as a student, but a spectator; he would encourage my trekking with him to the flats of dancers for whom he played his forever ambiguous role: part teacher, part tabla accompanist. I would sit on the expanse of mosaic floor that dancers favoured as their environment and determinedly keep time to the mostly sixteen-beat tala – teentaal. This was my way of consolidating my grasp of laya, or time, as the dancer practised complex permutations with stamps of her ankleted feet.

Layakari, or the display of rhythmic virtuosity (through the tattoo beaten out on the floor with the feet), is a major element in kathak dance. Hazarilalji ranked this as an element – despite the mastery it required – of secondary importance. 'Anyone can learn or do foot movement,' he'd say. 'In fact, that's all that dancers and students do these days! But not every dancer can do abhinaya.' This goes to the heart of this North Indian classical genre: kathak, derived from 'katha', or story. Abhinaya today commonly means 'acting'; but in kathak, it's a mode of storytelling through gesture. The stories are often to do with Radha's trysts with Krishna. The song narrating the story is the thumri, which itself is about Radha–Krishna's love, and whose name derives

165

from 'thumak', or the sound of the bells-wearing feet. Thumri's original function was to be sung to dance. It's an improvisational, rhythmically expansive form, not as unhurried as the khayal, but often set to a slow deep-chandi (or fourteen-beat cycle), a difficult measure to keep time to. In other words, the dancer doing abhinaya is released from the finite deadlines of 4/4 into something looser, into exploring the tentative but magic time of meeting Krishna. Before kathak (and other classical dance forms) went under temporarily with British rule, it – especially abhinaya – was refined by Wajid Ali Shah in his court in Awadh. Wajid Ali is portrayed as being too preoccupied with dance and poetry to notice, until it was too late, the machinations of the British, or to prevent the passing of his kingdom into their hands in 1856. But his place in the history of dance as a patron and innovator is certain; he was probably bisexual, which would explain his empathy for Radha over Krishna's absences.

To understand abhinaya, think of the movies of the silent era, where gesture and expression supersede image. Or look at the 'picturisation' of songs in the Hindi cinema of the late fifties and sixties, which eschews Broadway-style choreography for lassitude and facial close-ups. Abhinaya shows a path or journey through a hand gesture; surprise with the eyebrows. This is its way of recreating the world and our experience of living in it. Watching Hazarilalji demonstrate abhinaya, I saw him – a gaunt, long-haired man – as well as the universe he was making immediate. Both were visible. It seemed then that the European Renaissance's legacy – where, as on a great canvas or in a stage set, 'reality' is built detail by detail, brick by brick – was, for a form like abhinaya, irrelevant.

Hazarilalji did many things for me, but I was really beholden to him for taping thhekas – that is, the actual playing, at various tempos, of the talas – for me to take abroad. Prior to my departure, I'd start taping bandishes from Govindji – he even recorded these on his bed in his small new flat in Lonavla, when, after having fallen ill from an ischemic heart condition, he was recovering and had started teaching again: just his voice, no accompaniment, rendering the exquisite but bewilderingly difficult compositions of his father. I'd go to him with my Panasonic two-in-one and a cassette; the rest followed. Eve-of-departure measures, like hoarding rations before an emergency. Actually, I'd have spent the break taping each day: my guru's performances on All India Radio, if any were scheduled; Hindi film songs from the fifties and sixties, which I was discovering alongside – in discrete states of excitement – Elizabeth Bishop and the Irish poets in Paul Muldoon's *Faber Book of Contemporary Irish Poetry*.

I digress. Hazarilalji offered to record the slow (vilambit) twelve-beat ektaal and the fast (drut) sixteen-beat teentaal for me. He claimed to have the stamina; he was used to taping teentaal for dancers to practise their foot movement to. But to record slow ektaal over thirty or forty minutes (very slow, for me to expound on the alaap; slow, for me to develop the sargam, or the named notes of the raga, after the alaap was done; less slow, for me to move to rhythmic improvisation and taans), and then do the same for teentaal (less fast at first, to sing slow taans to; then fast, and faster) was an improbable feat. He switched the fan off to preclude its hiss; he allowed me to sit with him for a while, then indicated I was to close the door and go for a walk. When I returned, he was done, but I was concerned about his colour. In Warren Street, I began to practise to Hazarilalji's playing, which was less a recording than a document. It also carried in it St Cyril Road. A few times I played the cassette to listen for the sounds of the day that were audible behind the tabla.

In 1986, after graduating from UCL, I took a gap year in St Cyril Road. I became part of its flowering and decay, its burgeoning and decline. I loved how its poles of animation and rest sometimes became each other. There are very few genuine neighbourhoods; but, when you live in one, there's more to see in it than in the world. I kept going out for walks. I would go from St Cyril Road to contiguous lanes – St Leo, St Andrews, St Dominic, and St Anthony roads. Children ran past, pushing a wheel with a stick. The next day you'd find the wheel on the macadam. I found dogs napping, emulating the wheels, curled up in a circle.

It was a strange family, the Jaipurwales. When I say 'Jaipurwales', I include Hazarilalji; he'd married into the family, and adopted the surname – a reminder of his neither-here-nor-there status in life. In moments of pique with Govindji, he'd say his actual name was Hazarilal Sharma. The story was that he'd drifted into Bombay from nowhere and ingratiated himself with Laxman Prasad Jaipurwale. One day, Laxman Prasad decided Hazarilal would be his son-in-law.

When I say 'strange family', I mean its extraordinary gifts and achievements, and how little they meant in the end. So I mean 'strange world'. At the age of fifty-seven, I know that ignoring great talent isn't an aberration, but the norm; but my heart is a teenager's and still hasn't come to terms with this.

'Gharana' is the word used in North Indian classical music for a musical 'family', or school, or a set of characteristics associated with a style. Laxman Prasad's was called the Kunwar Shyam gharana. 'Kunwar Shyam', meaning the 'young' or 'unmarried' Shyam, or Krishna, is surely the pseudonym of the man who (two generations before Laxman Prasad) lived for a while in Delhi, composing bandishes and new variants of Malhar: Suha Malhar, Sughrai Malhar, Kafi Malhar, variants rarely heard outside extant recordings by Laxman and Govind Prasad Jaipurwale. The rains were to Kunwar Shyam what the 'inconstant wind' was to Shelley – 'The mind in creation is as a fading coal, which some invisible influence, like an inconstant wind, awakens to transitory brightness' – and his short compositions, set to teentaal, are the result. But the gharana's main repertoire comprises Laxman Prasad's compositions. Laxman Prasad was born in 1915 in Gujarat; he died in Bombay in 1977 (a year before Govindji entered our lives in Malabar Hill). He grew up in Jaipur, where his father was a court musician; I believe he was also interested in dance, something that's reflected in the unusual lyrics of his khayals, many of which describe moments in the lives of Radha and Krishna, and his compositions' unbelievably intricate rhythm patterns. Again and again, rhythmic and tonal virtuosity (layakari and taankari) converge in a way that's rare, if not unparalleled. Difficulty may be one of the reasons why this gharana has so few followers.

Laxman Prasad married a woman from a musical family whose maternal uncle, Khemchand Prakash, was a pioneering music composer in Hindi cinema, and who set to music the eerily beautiful songs of *Mahal* (1949). Laxman Prasad and Ganeshi Devi had two sons, Govind and Girdhar, and Chanda, a daughter. Both Govind and Girdhar learnt singing from their father. Girdharji once told me that Govind made such alarming progress that the younger brother felt there was no point in trying to keep up, and turned to the tabla.

A thin man in his portraits, Laxman Prasad had a bad heart and died at the age of sixty-two. At the time I was learning from Govindji, the family spoke of Laxman Prasad as if he belonged to another epoch, though the death was very recent and must have been fresh in their minds. One can only speculate about the kind of man he was. People called him a 'sant', or saint, possibly because of his simplicity and rejection of material needs; the brunt of this rejection was borne by the family. No one had a negative word to say about him. The rhythmic play of his compositions shows great intellectual powers; the melodic forms show not only mastery, but delicacy. Some of the lyrics, to do with Radha and Krishna, are sensuous and life-loving; others, as in a slow khayal in

Puriya Dhanashree, give evidence of the world-denying impulses people mentioned: 'Tohe laaj na awat re mana murakh / ka par karat guman' – 'Do you feel no shame, ignorant heart? / What makes you so full of yourself?'

Although Laxman Prasad had long-term students in Anima Roy (the flautist Pannalal Ghosh's niece) and Murli Manohar Shukla, and occasional ones like the late Manik Verma, his principal follower was Govindji. It was Govindji who had the gift, and the resolve, to be equal to the repertoire's demands; he had the original-ity to not obediently replicate his father's art. Oddly, it fell to me, a middle-class teenager, to become Govindji's main disciple, and to inherit several compositions of the Kunwar Shyam gharana. He had droves of other stu-dents, but they were all learning ghazals or bhajans. It's just that my meeting with Govindji coincided with my out-of-sync-with-the-world awakening to classical music. His talented son Bhavdeep was devoted to the ghazal; it was after Govindji's death that Bhavdeep began to amass, and learn from, his father's legacy.

Who knew Govindji would die so soon? I spent my gap year of 1986–87 in St Cyril Road. Govindji died in February 1988, when I was in Oxford. I crossed the road from Holywell Manor to the Martin Building in the evening, weeping; I was also angry: I believed Govindji had killed himself. He'd been blithe – about his diabetes; his heart condition. He was forty-four. In 1989, my parents sold the flat in Bandra and moved to Calcutta. Bombay was over. Hazarilalji died in the mid-nineties. For these reasons, St Cyril Road has an air for me of both overture and epilogue, of fresh beginnings, rapid endings. I started a novel in that gap year. I learnt regularly from Govindji, alongside Girdharji and Hazarilalji. The world was close at hand: from the dining-room window, I saw a cuckoo eating a gulmohar flower.

Govindji sang the ghazal because he loved the form. But, in the eighties, it was also the bitcoin of popular Indian music. The ghazal is the Urdu love lyric; it originates in Persian, but has an extraordinary centuries-old history in Urdu. In the eighties, it had a revival in India for three reasons. The first had to do with a renaissance of the form in Pakistan. The Pakistani revival preceded General Zia-ul-Haq's Islamisation campaign, his religio-political antipathy to music for being un-Islamic, and the subsequent banishing of classical music in Pakistan partly for its perceived Hindu content. This resulted in the enriching, in Zia's dystopia, of the sensibility of Mehdi Hassan. What's often said about Hassan may be true: that he was by temperament a classical musician, but, given the increasing aridity (from before Zia's time) of the classical terrain in Pakistan, he brought something of the khayal's tonal depth and expansiveness to the ghazal. Hassan's ghazals started making their way to Bombay in the seventies.

The second reason was the death, in the eighties, of the richest popular music tradition in post-Independence India – Hindi film music. The strangulation of experimentation in film music – its unfettered references and registers; its soundscape, which foresaw and rivalled, from the late fifties, Western pop in 1967 – was caused by the same thing that contributed to new lushly arranged ghazal parodies: the dominance of the market. The market is the third reason. It frowned on individuality in music composition in Hindi cinema, probably because originality implies risk, leading, in the characteristic paradoxes of free-market wisdom, to the film songs of the eighties becoming commercial disasters. On the other hand, taking advantage of the Mehdi Hassan upsurge and addressing the void left by the film song, music companies began promoting not artists but ghazal-substitutes sung by canny, second-rate singers. A hostility to judgement and sensibility came into being, whose legacy we're experiencing today not only in art, but in politics.

Each time we departed the pastoral of St Cyril Road for the Bombay I'd grown up in – as we did every day, from a sense of duty – we'd see from the car large hoardings on which the faces of the new ghazal singers were advertised. Celebrity was power; you felt diminished by it. Rubbish singers in regalia were our dictators. Govindji was lost. He too made that journey from the north to the south of the city. He knew the singers, and would have had to contemplate the billboards. I saw a faraway look in his eyes more than once. Despite his mastery of the ghazal, he could make little headway with it, except teaching it to a rich clientele; he was an anachronism in the eighties – an artist. His astonishing accomplishment, his riyaaz, as a classical singer hadn't got him far, maybe because he was an outsider from a Rajasthani family that had moved to Bombay. His bafflement – about his *purpose* – is fairly familiar to me, as a writer of the present, as it would be to others in the arts today.

When my parents left St Cyril Road and Bombay, packing (crates full of books and china and even records) overwhelmed any sense of lingering over. We'd had enough of debt (the flat had had to be sold); and I was tired of Bombay's ostentation, its ostentatious unreflectiveness. I urged my parents to go. Govindji's death too was a departure of a kind. He'd seen the failure of his father's attempts to reject materialism; he pursued another path; he pursued the ghazal, forced to put the khayal on the back burner. I saw his death as an inability to come to terms, and make peace, with the India that was then coming into existence.

In 1999, I returned to Calcutta from England, fatigued by what Blairism was doing to television, newspapers, bookshops, and cities.

2
Modernism and
the Khayal

The khayal first entered the Mughal court in the reign of Emperor Jahangir (1605–27) via qawwali singers of the Sufi sect. But to get a sense of the particular form of the khayal that is in circulation among practitioners today, we must go back to the eighteenth century and the court of the emperor Muhammad Shah (1702–48), a ruler accused of bad governance and degeneracy, but deemed as well to be an exceptional patron of the arts. Muhammad Shah represents the extinction of Mughal rule; Nader Shah of Persia defeated his army in battle and sacked Delhi in 1739, dealing an Achilles-like blow to the Mughal Empire from which it didn't recover. Muhammad Shah died in 1748. In 1757, the East India Company won the Battle of Plassey (palashir juddha) in Bengal with the help of the traitorous general Mir Jafar, and gained a decisive grip on India.

But Muhammad Shah was also known as 'sada rangile', the 'perpetually colourful' or 'perpetually joyous': 'sada' from the Sanskrit 'sadaira', or 'eternally'; 'rangile', a derivation from 'rang', a term descended from both Sanskrit and Persian, meaning 'colour', but also 'brightness', 'redness', or 'joy'. This speaks to Muhammad Shah's imagination-embracing side. In that doomed but clearly exuberant milieu lived the two court musicians to whom is attributed the innovation of the khayal form, and whose compositions, often managing to accommodate genuine spiritual emotion alongside their homage to the emperor's court, are sung today by most khayal singers. The first was Niyamat Khan, better known through his songs as 'Sadarang', which is almost the same word, and means the same thing, as 'sadarangile'. Niyamat's nephew Feroz Khan, or 'Adarang', was the second composer and songwriter. 'Ada' in Arabic means 'grace'.

It's argued that the root of the Sanskrit 'raga' is probably 'rang'. By adopting the pseudonyms Sadarang and Adarang, Niyamat Khan and Feroz Khan were locating themselves in an imaginative tradition in which creativity is made synonymous with a transformed mood: of colour, emotional richness and range, and joy – maybe celebration. The divagations of khayal – Arabic for the 'imagination', but also, in Urdu, 'thought', 'idea', even 'whim' – are always dependent on a particular mood being in place. The word 'mood' has been imported into Indian languages and into casual discussions of classical music to describe a state that enables exploration and elaboration: 'Woh aaj mood mein nahin thhe' – 'He wasn't in the mood today'; or 'Bahut mood mein hain!', meaning 'He's in great form!' Here, what 'mood' acknowledges is the primacy of the creative state over accomplishment when it comes to performance, as well as that state's contingency: it can't be taken for granted. 'Mood' is part of the same lexicon as 'rang' and 'khayal', each, in turn, related to 'raga'. The vocabulary is inadvertently synaesthetic, as are concepts like 'the blues' and 'mood indigo'. 'Mood' has to do with the freedom creative facilitation brings.

The khayal is a development on an earlier form called the dhrupad. The word comes from a combination of the Sanskrit 'dhruva', the word for 'steadfast' and 'unchanging', often used of the North Star, and 'pada', meaning 'poem' or 'verse'. 'Pada' is also Sanskrit for 'foot', and therefore 'measure' or 'metre'; it's part of the Indo-European family – 'pedes' is Latin for 'feet'. The matter of scansion – 'pada' – is pertinent here, given the emphasis on repeated, long-drawn-out rhythmic play in dhrupad exposition.

The dhrupad possibly goes back to the eleventh century, or even further back, but its key practitioners can be traced back to the fifteenth. Of these, the best known is the poet–sage–singer Swami Haridas, who's said to have taught the form to Tansen and his rival Baiju Bawra. In its devotional content and its majestic preoccupation with laya, or rhythmic progression, dhrupad bears some resemblance to the Carnatic or classical tradition of the South.

The dhrupad is accompanied by the pakhawaj, a drum that's placed horizontally on the lap and played on either side with each hand. The right side is narrower than the left. The pakhawaj is somewhat like a joined-up tabla, or, more accurately, the tabla (since it comes later) like a split-into-two pakhawaj, the halves like the pairs in Aristophanes' story that yearn to merge into each other, but can't. The tabla gives the khayal rhythmic accompaniment, and produces more complex permutations, and has greater tonal range, than not only the pakhawaj, but any percussion instrument.

The tradition of Hindustani classical music is a history of creative (and critical) interfaces – between a lineage that goes back to Vedic chants, to a system recorded by Bharata, encompassing melodic elaborations and singular talas, to a fineness and previously unheard virtuosity imparted to it over time by Muslim culture. The role of birthplace or region shouldn't be discounted. The vocal style of a singer from Dharwad, on the edge of 'South India', will have echoes of Carnatic modulations; a Punjabi classical vocalist is likely to use grace notes common to the region's folk music.

Before the dhrupadiya embarks on the composition and the pakhawaj player starts to slap out the talas, he – it's almost always 'he'; there are relatively few women dhrupad singers, though numbers have been growing – expands on the raga in a 'nom tom' alaap. The pakhawaj stays quiet during this long 'introduction'; the nom tom alaap is a kind of soliloquy, a journey undertaken alone – maybe even in solitude, as neither audience nor accompanist is required. The singer ascends towards the upper tonic using the syllables 'nom' and 'tom'. An illusion of a 4/4 time signature is sometimes maintained, to create momentum: not a strict temporality, but one that's loosely woven in and out of the syllabic repetition. What do 'nom' and 'tom' – and additional sounds like 'ta na na na' – mean? On the one hand, they replicate the plucked sound of the strings of the veena and the sitar. The 'nom tom' alaap is very akin to the sitar's jhala, played in bursts of 4/4 before the actual composition starts with tabla accompaniment. There's also a proximity to 'om'. 'Om' means 'nothing': 'nothing' as plenitude. In the dhrupad's nom tom beginnings, we're in a domain – and this is something that the khayal takes further, especially in the twentieth century – where speech is sound rather than 'meaning' in a conventional sense. With the khayal, by the twenties, we're witnessing a radical non-representational shift whose inclinations are modernist. Ustad Abdul Wahid Khan's experiments with khayal early on in the last century and Eliot's suggestion in 1932 that 'Genuine poetry can communicate before it is understood' aren't miles apart in their tendencies.

What do I mean by 'modernist'? The word has many meanings, but I'm thinking of something specific: the destruction of recognisability. In literature, for instance, we distinguish a short story from a poem through features marking out their respective forms. A song has a form too; a shape; a beginning and end. It's recognisable as a song through its form's representational qualities. In art and writing, form is also involved in representing reality: say, colours and lines in a painting making a bull or a mountain.

In Turner's paintings of water, and particularly in his *Rain, Steam and Speed* from 1844, we have a dissolution of recognisability, of the reliably identifiable. The painting is awash with modulations on emptiness. It's a prolepsis of what in the twentieth century would be called 'abstract art'. In focusing on intangibles, or the tangible becoming intangible – an oncoming train seen in terms of 'Rain, Steam and Speed' – it exemplifies, early on, modernism's acute need to be free of the representational.

Claude Monet immersed himself in his obsession with the pond of water lilies early in the last century – roughly between 1915 and his death in 1927. Not only did he, in more than one sense, lose perspective (which had given to neoclassical painting its rationalist, photographic air of order and reality), so that the viewer in the Musée de l'Orangerie is often unable to tell lily apart from water, or water from bank – he seemed to have given up on the idea that each painting is a separate occasion. Instead, he set about repeating the same work, proving, at once, that repeating the same work is out of the question.

The turn from representation takes place first in Maharaja Man Singh's court in Jodhpur in 1823. I felt the faintest inkling of this when I visited the *Garden and Cosmos* exhibition at the British Museum in 2009. The paintings in what the curators called the 'Cosmos' section of the exhibition were astonishing. They seem to me now the first attempts – certainly, the earliest attempts I have seen – to qualify the human figure, and pay greater attention to what we call 'background': emptiness not as lack, but its opposite.

These paintings were commissioned because Man Singh fell under the spell of the Nath yogis and their pursuit of a formless Absolute. He wanted to behold this Absolute in painting, and the artist Bulaki responded in 1823 by placing the figure of a yogi in the centre, and creating, around him, an expanse of dull gold. In another painting, the yogi is seated in exactly the same manner on grey rock, the gold sheen behind him; in a third painting, he's gone, as if in a vanishing trick: only the gold expanse remains. The three paintings form a panel, with pure emptiness on the extreme left; the yogi floating in radiance in the centre; and the picture of him seated on grey matter on the extreme right. They can be seen as a sequence, but I prefer each as a fresh reverie. Gold was used because it's a pure metal, but also because its glow is understated. The nothingness is neither fully present nor absent.

Bulaki also painted Nath yogis seated in the midst of what the curators called 'cosmic oceans', which either shimmer, like tinfoil, or display whorls, like finger-prints. These works look towards Monet's departures from representation, via water, a century later, just as Monet makes possible the scenes in Jean Renoir's *Partie de campagne*, where, for minutes, there's little but river and riverbank, in a long, baffling take, as well as, later, shots of rain on the water, creating a gooseflesh akin to Bulaki's fingerprints.

Man Singh's tenure wasn't an easy one. On the death of his father, his claim to the throne was challenged – successfully – by his cousin Bheem Singh. Man Singh returned to power in 1803, defeating Bheem Singh in an exhausting, protracted battle in which he held his nerve, apparently with the sustenance and advice of his spiritual advisers, the ascetics of the Nath yogi sect. During his reign, Man Singh concentrated on deepening his understanding of hatha yoga, often through art and music, to an unusual and, for his court, alarming degree. He signed a treaty with the British on 6 January 1818, and died in 1843 – fourteen years before the British Crown took charge of India from the East India Company.

It's striking that three kings under whose patronage some of the most important developments in the arts took place – Man Singh and the beginnings, in modernity, of non-figurative art; Muhammad Shah Rangile and the khayal; Wajid Ali Shah of Awadh and the refining of the thumri and kathak dance – should also stand for the last breath of the old order and its fatal weakening. At least two – Muhammad Shah and Wajid Ali Shah – would have been characterised, for colonialist historians, by 'decadence'; they seemingly allowed, while they were preoccupied with 'decadent' art forms, the British to come in. Yet it's also possible to see them as moderns, prefiguring Thomas Mann's conception of the modern as an artist and daydreamer who fails to uphold, and swerves away from, the bourgeois inheritance left to him by the father. About his semi-autobiographical creation, the writer Tonio Kröger, Mann's narrator has this to say in the eponymous story: 'The old Kröger family gradually declined, and some people quite rightly considered Tonio Kröger's own existence and way of life as one of the signs of decay.' Something similar is happening in the nineteenth century on the cusp of colonialism, among minor kings and emperors who are also key patrons of the arts, midwives to major imaginative shifts, and irresponsible rulers. Colonialism is facilitated; but the ground is also being created for a new modernity.

Contemporaneous and comparable instances can be found in a non-feudal setting, in Calcutta, related both to colonialism and, in tension with it, to the birth-passage of the modern. 'Prince' Dwarkanath Tagore (1794–1846) made his money in his dealings with the Company and as a landowner. With his son Debendranath (1817–1905) began the process of turning away from this legacy and bringing into being a different one: Debendranath was a philosopher and founder of the Brahmo Samaj. The Samaj, created by Rammohun Roy (1772–1833) and Debendranath, is identified with pathbreaking social reform; but its engagement, especially after Debendranath's rediscovery of the Upanishads, with a niraakar, immanent Absolute – that is, an Absolute without outline or form – connects it with, at once, the Nath yogis, the artist Bulaki in Man Singh's court, and Flaubert's observation that the author should be like God in the universe, 'everywhere present, but nowhere visible'. Debendranath's Tonio Kröger-like turn is deepened in his son, the poet Rabindranath, through whom, along with Mallarmé, the non-representational begins to enter poetry. These are contexts in which we must also place the khayal.

A raga is not a mode. That is, it isn't a linear movement. It's a simultaneity of notes, a constellation, in a way quite different from harmony. Of course, harmony can be linear and modal – the C major chord is followed by the F major chord, which leads to G major. A departure from this development signals a break in linear harmonic progression. With a raga, one doesn't think in these terms. One isn't even positing the melodic against the harmonic. One is exploring simultaneity in a particular way. For instance, the singer singing the note pa (that is, the fifth) in Yaman is aware at each moment of its peculiar relationship to re, or the second; as is the audience. But it's not as if the re is necessarily sounded, as it would be in a chord. It's held in suspension – but it exists as a constant presence, as well as an available route: it, and its relationship to the fifth, could be invoked at any moment. The singer also knows that the glissando between pa and re isn't the same as an identical one in Chhaya Nat. The difference arises from the specific sets of notes that distinguish Yaman from Chhaya Nat. What we have in a raga is an interrelationship, a balance, pointing not so much to melody, but to a way (distinct from harmony) of thinking about the juxtaposition of notes.

189

A raga in a khayal is a melody slowed down to an extent that the simultaneity and potential relationship between notes, and the emotional weight and texture of each note, supersedes melodic form. If you sing the raga as a song, or a drut bandish, a fast-tempo composition, it will be audible as a song. But if you dilate and expand it, as in the alaap of a slow khayal, the song-like incarnation of the raga becomes impossible to pinpoint for the lay ear. The listener not attuned to classical music is in the same place as the puzzled viewers of the water lilies in the Orangerie were in 1920.

The khayal singer credited with this slowing down is Ustad Abdul Wahid Khan, who was born in 1871 in Kirana in Uttar Pradesh, India, and died in Lahore, Pakistan, in 1949. The Ustad's love of the spiritual, of Sufism, meant he had few ambitions as a court singer, performed little in public, and resisted being recorded. There are few surviving recordings except the ones that were done surreptitiously. Wahid Khan retarded mid-tempo time signatures to half their speed, so that he might explore the raga without any sense of shacklement. This happened early in the twentieth century. Among those impacted by Wahid Khan's style and experiment was the young Ustad Amir Khan, the most influential khayal singer of the last century, who largely gave to the form the slow (to some, bewildering) meditative and digressive quality that marks it out today. Ustad Amir Khan wasn't a student of Abdul Wahid Khan, but he saw the opening the latter had created, and opened it up further. He slowed down the vilambit khayal to four times its previous duration. His preferred tala (or time signature) for alaap was the fourteen-beat jhoomra (which means 'to sway to'), a lively measure, as the name suggests, when played at a normal tempo. The first listeners of Amir Khan's tabla player's jhoomra wouldn't have recognised the tala at all; in fact, there were complaints that the meaning of the name of the tala had seemingly little to do with it after its metamorphosis. This retardation reshaped other talas too, including the one used most commonly today in vilambit khayal: ektaal.

Ektaal is a twelve-beat tala. I'm going to write out the bols of the tala below. A bol is a syllable or, literally, utterance: it refers to the range of sounds tapped out by the fingers and palm on the tabla. The word is a reminder of the non-anthropomorphic world of Hindustani classical music, in which utterance is not necessarily related to human speech and meaning-making, but is any sound produced by a living thing or object. Ektaal's allocation of bols over its twelve beats is:

1	2	3	4	5	6	7	8
dhin	dhin	dha ge	ti ra ka ta	tun	na	ka	ta

9	10	11	12
dha ge	ti ra ka ta	dhin	na na

Post-Amir Khan, the beats are multiplied by four, so that each beat takes up approximately four seconds. A time-cycle that, played at medium-fast tempo, lasts about twelve seconds (one second per beat), and in fast tempo maybe six seconds, takes a minute or more to complete in vilambit khayal. To give an accurate impression of the effect this has, I'm writing the bols of ektaal again, but this time with one beat occupying one page. As you read each page, count out four seconds, including the bol(s), before turning the page. In your head, multiply this experience by thirty minutes. This might give you a sense of what Ustad Amir Khan did to alaap.

(1   2   3   4)

dhin

(1   2   3   4)

dhin

(1   2   3   4)

dha   ge

(1	2	3	4)
ti	ra	ka	ta

(1   2   3   4)

tun

(1   2   3   4)

na

(1 2 3 4)

ka

(1   2   3   4)

ta

(1   2   3   4)

dha   ge

(1	2	3	4)
ti	ra	ka	ta

(1   2   3   4)

dhin

(1   2   3   4)

na   na

Blankness dominates the last twelve pages, but the pages to contemplate are the ones that say 'dhin', 'tun', 'na', 'ka', and 'ta'. These are where one bol or syllable is struck to signify one beat in the twelve-beat cycle. At this unnaturally vilambit speed, three seconds of silence elapse (1 + 3 = 4; each beat, as I said before, is multiplied by four, and lasts four seconds or more) after the bol is played and before the next one arrives. Some tabla players will fill out 'tun' or 'na' with an extra beat or two, but others will pause so that everything seems to stop for a short but noticcable period. We hear 'dhin', then ponder something like a page left almost entirely blank. This is not a chasm. Its precursor is the gold sheen in Bulaki's 1823 paintings. One could keep in mind also the longueurs in the forty-minute-long alaap-length *Partie de campagne*, of water, rain, and sky, when the camera moves but the narrative stops in the way the fingers do after 'dhin'. These – the slowed-down ektaal; Bulaki's expanse of gold; Renoir's short film – are artworks that declare their meaning through caesuras.

It required courage and single-mindedness on Ustad Amir Khan's part to slow down talas to a point where they could no longer be plausible representations of themselves. Nor is a raga sung at this speed anything close to a 'normal' portrait of a raga. The tabla keeps 4/4 time, but while the duration of 4/4 is generally four beats, here, the cycle, stretched to forty-eight beats, has a horizon that, as the khayal begins, seems far off. The port is the one in the cycle. Until you approach the port, you sing in free time, maybe exploring, at first, two or three notes. So two temporalities unfold in the alaap: the time kept by the tabla player (let's say one, two, three, four per beat) and the unmoored time of the singing. Only as they come closer to the one (by the end of the eleventh beat in ektaal) does the singer return to the composition and to 4/4, and arrive at the port (the sama, or one) with an appointed word in the composition. Each khayal composition gives to one word the job of hitting the sama: say, if the first line is 'Hari ke naam le lo' ('Speak Hari's name'), the word 'naam' might be that word. For forty-four seconds or so, the singer explores two notes, or three, or four or more (depending on where they are in the raga). At approximately forty seconds, the port is visible again. They disembark briefly, with emphasis: 'Hari ke *naam*' – through 'naam' alighting on the one. Then, the next moment, the tala cycle repeats itself, and the singer has once more taken to sea.

I was practising recently with my accompanists in the afternoon when the tabla player, Ashok, took a gulp of water mid-vilambit from the bottle he keeps near him when he plays. I too broke from the khayal, though both he and the harmonium player continued playing, to say: 'You realise you could do that only because Abdul Wahid Khan and Amir Khan slowed down the talas

206

so much?' He laughed loudly, but later we discussed, semi-seriously, the conditions that made that swig of water possible. 'I could do it with the bols after which the tabla player needn't play another beat until some time has elapsed – but it *also* needs to be a beat which I'm only playing with one hand.' For instance, there's a useful gap after dhin, but you have to create that sound – which has, simultaneously, a ringing sharp tone as well as a deep bass one – with the fingers of both hands, the right-hand tabla producing the high-pitched ring, the left-hand one the boom. 'Tun', 'na', 'ka', and 'ta' can all be created with the right hand alone. So:

the sixth beat of ektaal

(1   2   3   4)

tun

gives Ashok barely enough time (as he pointed out to me) to play it with the left hand, unscrew the bottle top with the right, take that swig of water, and return to the next beat, na.

(A word about 'dhin'.

As I've just said, it takes a finger on the baya – literally, the 'left', the large tabla – and one hitting the tabla on the right simultaneously to create this bol. The finger on the baya can press down on the membrane to create not only the bass boom but to prolong it tonally, so that it seems to draw itself out and rise upwards:

$$n - n - n$$
$$- n - n -$$
$$dhin - n - n$$

This may be the only instance in music of a percussive sound, and a drum, producing a bent note, or meend.)

Other signs of modernism in khayal include:

1 Frequent indifference to the meaning of the
  composition's words. Words are for melodic
  improvisation, to explore the upward and downward
  journey (arohan and avarohan) through the raga's notes.
  Any word can serve this purpose; a syllable will do.
  Meaning is marginalised. (I've heard that Ustad Amir
  Khan, when asked what words he hummed to, replied:
  'My telephone number, sometimes.') Words might also
  be used in rhythmic play in a way little different from
  a nonsense sound like 'nom' or 'tom' or 'ta na'. And, of
  course, a chosen word returns the exposition repeatedly
  to the one of the time cycle. Here, again, a syllable is
  enough, and the names of gods get no more respect than
  other words. If it's the first syllable of 'Hari' that's to
  land on the sama, then the singer may sing 'Ha' with
  power and mumble the 'ri'. Modernism, in contrast to
  the devotional temper, has a spiritual timbre which arises
  not from meaning, but sound.

2 A singer might interrupt a performance because the
  tanpura is fractionally off-pitch. Classical musicians
  depend on the tanpura's tonic and on the string playing

the interval to navigate the raga. So the strings need to be true. A tabla player too might bring proceedings to a halt to knock diligently on the right-hand tabla (tuned to the sa) because its pitch has strayed slightly. In no other kind of music, not Indian, Western, pop, jazz, or even Carnatic, are we witness to such a break. The khayal asks us not to distinguish between process and finished product.

3 The tuning of instruments – the tanpura, the tabla, or (if it's an instrumental performance) the sitar's strings – might be pursued indefinitely before the performance starts. The curtain goes up, but the musicians' namaskar to the audience may not mark a beginning. At George Harrison's Concert for Bangladesh in 1971, the audience applauded when Ravi Shankar and his accompanists paused after tuning, as if they'd been privy to an obscure experiment. Ravi Shankar said, 'If you liked the tuning so much, I hope you'll like the music too.' So the North Indian classical recital sets aside – in comparison to other traditions – the requirement for a well-defined starting-point ('riverrun', the first word of *Finnegans Wake*, is also a continuation of the book's incomplete final sentence). It shows a greater indifference to the separation between green-room 'warming up' and the 'official' recital than we're used to.

Here, I should mention *ni*, or the lower seventh: the note leading to the tonic, or sa. All musical traditions recognise, I'd hazard, that the seventh in the middle octave is a leading note, seeking completion in the upper tonic. But what of *ni*? You notice, even when the composition is being sung and the time cycle has been entered, how long the singer stays at the margin of the lower *ni* in their elaborations, touching it, dipping further below, then once more climbing to it without embracing the tonic. What's going on here? It's a sort of submerged broaching of the nascent, the prenatal. The performance has begun, but the tonic, the raga's starting-point, hasn't been arrived at. The singer might *hint* at what a beginning and its subsequent progression might look like: that is, they might sing the *ni*, touch the re, or the middle octave's second note, and then return to *ni*, all the while avoiding the sa. This is to say: I'm emerging into the light, but am still unborn. The lower *ni* then begins to feel like not only what happens *before* we start, but the coming to an end of *something else*. As with 'riverrun', what creates the distinction between end and start is being put to one side.

4 A singer might clear their throat from time to time, to get rid of phlegm, or a cough. The khayal allows for fresh beginnings and drafts. Decades ago, certain ustads reportedly kept spittoons at their side. Hazarilalji used to call the great Faiyaz Khan of the Agra gharana 'aak thhoo' for his (according to Hazarilalji) frequent use of the spittoon. Faiyaz Khan was long dead when I was

told this, so I can't confirm its accuracy. But almost every khayal singer has cleared their throat at some point during a concert. There's a beauty to this brief struggle. Impediments to immersion must be banished, but there's no guarantee they'll be removed before the concert starts. The concert is an attempt at immersion; impediments are dealt with as they occur.

There is in Hindustani classical performance – in khayal, especially – an eccentricity arising from formal preoccupations. There's also an expectation that the audience will be patient: not only with the circumlocutory, but with the strange. Process over artefact is a modernist preference.

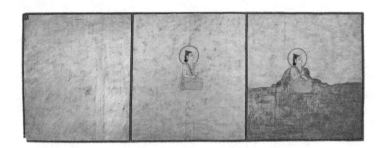

It's said that Indian classical music is improvisational. But what's meant by 'improvisation'? There's no word in the Indian languages that corresponds exactly with the term or idea. There's 'alankaar' and 'sringaar', meaning 'elaboration' and 'ornamentation'. 'Sringaar' is part of the vocabulary of kathak dance: it refers to a woman (possibly Radha) doing her toilette. She's preparing to meet her lover (possibly Krishna). The dancer's gestures enacting sringaar (adorning herself) converge with the idea that 'making up', make-believe, and the gestures of improvisation are inherent in everyday practices. Radha's sringaar, in kathak, is a manifestation of abhinaya's urge to adorn, to develop on; but I've also heard musicians speak of elaboration in khayal or thumri – that is, singing a phrase in two or three different ways – as 'sringaar'.

There's no word for improvisation because improvisation *is* music; the fact that music could be otherwise would have been news to an eighteenth-century performer in India.

In Hindustani classical music, improvisation is deferral.

If a raga is a cluster of progressions and interrelationships, I, as a performer, will delay – without disfiguring the raga's form – a straightforward portrayal of these interrelationships for as long as possible. If I'm supposed to ascend the notes of Yaman and then return to the sa in this way – *ni* re ga re sa – I will procrastinate, maybe singing *ni* re ga *ni, ni* re *ni, ni* re ga re ga re sa. If I'm to ascend the sharp fourth, returning to the tonic like this – *ni* re ga re má ga re sa – I might sing *ni* re ga re má ga re, ni re ga re sa instead. I'll delay the expected; the audience will await the expected but partake intensely of the delay. I won't come to the point. My not coming to the point will be synonymous with the pleasure of improvisation.

People have asked me, 'In what way does being a musician affect your writing?'; or, 'Is the form of your novel *Afternoon Raag* based on the raga?' I've evaded these questions as I don't have an answer. Feebly, I repeat what's true: I don't remember I'm a singer when I write. I don't remember I'm a writer when I sing. But, after three decades, I see at least one link: I'm told I have a tendency not to come to the point. Some Indian critics, in particular, have taken me to task for this. The Anglophone Indian, in the last thirty years, has been impatient with digression, unless it's connected to identity: 'We Indians always digress.' Going off point as a means to seeking beauty isn't of interest, although that's what improvisation in Hindustani classical music is.

When I was writing my first novel between 1986 and 1988, I invoked a parallel with improvisation without knowing it. I was describing a walk taken in Calcutta by a man with his two sons and his nephew from Bombay during a power cut in the evening. The nephew, Sandeep, is drawn to the semi-visible houses; the narrator knows already that Sandeep's distraction is bound to frustrate a certain kind of reader:

But why did these houses – for instance, that one with the tall, ornate iron gates and a watchman dozing on a stool, which gave the impression that the family had valuables locked away inside, or that other one with the small porch and the painted door, which gave the impression that whenever there was a feast or a wedding all the relatives would be invited, and there would be so many relatives that some of them, probably the young men and women, would be sitting bunched together on the cramped porch because there would be no more space inside, talking eloquently about something that didn't really require eloquence, laughing uproariously at a joke that wasn't really very funny, or this next

house with an old man relaxing in his easy-chair on
the verandah, fanning himself with a local Sunday
newspaper, or this small, shabby house with the girl
Sandeep glimpsed through a window, sitting in a bare,
ill-furnished room, memorising a text by candlelight,
repeating suffixes and prefixes from a Bengali grammar
over and over to herself – why did these houses seem
to suggest that an infinitely interesting story might be
woven around them? And yet the story would never be
a satisfying one, because the writer, like Sandeep, would
be too caught up in jotting down the irrelevances and
digressions that make up lives, and the life of a city,
rather than a good story – till the reader would shout
'Come to the point!' – and there would be no point,
except the girl memorising the rules of grammar, the
old man in the easy-chair fanning himself, and the
house with the small, empty porch which was crowded,
paradoxically, with many memories and possibilities. The
'real' story, with its beginning, middle and conclusion,
would never be told, because it did not exist.

Those less in sympathy with khayal may cry, 'Come to
the point!'; but those acquainted with alaap see evasion
as the principal activity of creation.

Laya and tala – temporality and time signature – give to both Hindustani classical and Carnatic music a difficulty, beauty, and contained excitement that has no parallel in any other musical system. Let's see if I can give the reader a brief sketch of the bases of tala and layakari.

The commonest tala, or time signature, in Hindustani classical music is teentaal. It has sixteen beats: 4 × 4. The 4/4 metre is basic to all rhythm; but, turned into a cycle of sixteen accommodating the span of each line in a composition, the 4/4 gains dignity of form. Teentaal accompanies bandishes in mid-tempo and fast laya, though Maharashtrian khayal singers do often slow it down for the purposes of vilambit khayal. I'm putting down teentaal's syllables below, juxtaposing them with the first line of a composition by Laxman Prasad Jaipurwale in raga Purvi ('badi badi ankhiyan mein kajara sohe', which means 'kohl rests on large eyes').

1	2	3	4	/	5	6	7	8	/
na	dhin	dhin	na		na	dhin	dhin	na	

9	10	11	12 /	13	14	15	16 /
na	tin	tin	na	na	dhin	dhin	na
ba - - - di		*ba - - - di*		*an - - - khi - - - ya - - - na*			

1	2	3	4 /	5	6	7	8 /
na	dhin	dhin	na	na	dhin	dhin	na
mein ---------		*ka - - - ja - - - ra -----------*				*so - - - he*	

The syllables of 'badi badi ankhiyan mein kajara sohe' are distributed over the sixteen-beat cycle, so that the word 'mein' ('in' or 'on', from 'kohl rests *on* large eyes') is the word that must return to the sama, the one, whatever departures otherwise take place.

Virtuosic play – layakari – with the tala comprises permutations, calculations, slowing down or increasing the tempo to one and a half, two, or three times the original speed, and a set of triplets called tihai – that is, three sets of identical beats – at the end, whose last beat must land on the one. Layakari is meant to excite as well as confuse, by introducing a rhythmic difficulty where it becomes a struggle for the listener to maintain, or even remember, the original tempo and cycle during the virtuosic spell. It's also meant to raise the question – how, after the improvisatory excursion, is the tabla player going to get back to the sama? The improviser invents a problem in order to offer a solution – that's one way of looking at layakari. Its foundations are mathematical.

Let's look at the most basic permutation on teentaal, a triplet that can, of course, be complicated infinitely. (If you wish, you can keep count on your fingers – sixteen beats in mid-tempo; say, half a second per beat; and the triplet in double time.) The triplet comprises three clusters of five played at double tempo, where the first two clusters have a silent additional sixth beat: so 123456, 123456, 12345. If you include the two silent sixth beats, the three triplets add up to seventeen in all: $5+(1) + 5+(1) + 5 = 17$. Keep in mind that a sixteen-beat cycle, played at double tempo, would accommodate *two* cycles of sixteen: thirty-two beats. If you play seventeen beats at double tempo after half (eight beats) of the cycle is through, the seventeenth should inevitably arrive at the one.

1	2	3	4 /	5	6	7	8 /
9	10	11	12 /	13	14	15	16 /
$(1 - 2 - 3 - 4 - 5)$, 6		$(1 - 2 - 3 - 4 - 5)$, 6		$(1 - 2 - 3 - 4 -$			

1	2	3	4 /	5	6	7	8 /
5)							

Layakari asks performer and listener to do two things at once – be faithful to the original tempo; participate in the aberration until the percussionist finds an elegant way of coming back. It asks a third thing: to admire both the departure and the return.

When I say, 'Keep count with your fingers,' I don't mean fingertips, but the creases each digit has: three, plus fingertip, add up to four points for counting. Four fingers, excluding the thumb (never used), give you sixteen marks: one cycle of teentaal. This is how you keep time in Hindustani classical music when you're following layakari in detail. The sixteen creases mean as much to a musician as your palm's lines do to an astrologer.

An instrumentalist or tabla player may plan their departures and returns with elaborate, already-prepared pieces, but a singer might, depending on their mastery, devise something on the spot, jumping out of the cycle and back into it. Layakari courts danger. You may not make it safely to the one.

Rhythm in modern Western music is largely the contribution of Africans and Latin Americans. The 4/4 in rock or funk elicits a mild but vigorous nod, and a rhythmic abutment of the chin or recurrent head-butt. The body, in its ennui, moves backwards and forwards.

The ecstasy of layakari produces stillness. There's no metronomic head movement because the improviser has moved far away from the composition's tempo. Instead, the listener, if they're educated in laya, and if they're brave, may adhere to the original tempo with claps. Each time signature has a set number of claps; the word 'tala' or 'taal', meaning 'beat', is related to 'tali' or 'clap'. Teentaal has three: on the first, fifth, and thirteenth beats. I say 'brave' because it's a challenge holding the tempo in the face of an improvisation. The horse rears; you hang on; you want it to rear because therein lies the beauty you're trying to grasp. The head's stillness comes from trying to stay calm and immovable with the original time signature on which there's a burst of mathematical play. It also comes from catching your breath as you anticipate return.

3
Ah-nanda

From my mother I unwittingly inherited the template that the singing voice must be pitch-perfect, saturated in sur, and that it must be calm. As a child, I took this to be 'normal'. Calm and tonal richness attracted me, and, through my mother's example, went hand in hand.

Not that she was calm. As a child, I preferred my father's company: a very patient man. Handsome, too. My mother was excitable. She threw a bunch of keys to the floor in a fit of rage. Her anger died very soon, coming, going, as inspiration does. The next moment she'd be happy. She did a number of things to excess: get angry; laugh; consume sweet things.

There was no relation between her vocal style and her temperament.

Her voice and singing were transcendental. This is a suspect word, and I don't mean 'unworldly' by it. I mean her style – in a productive way – rejected emotion.

She told me a couple of times when I was about twenty-one or twenty-two that singing should be like speaking. She was arguing with the idea that it should be consciously 'different', a mode of heightened self-expression. Speaking doesn't draw undue attention to the self, or to the act of speaking. We forget the effort it's taken us to learn how to speak, and the skill involved. Speaking is as much a forgetting of the self as it has to do with self-disclosure. I think my mother was hinting at the forget-fulness that's necessary for, and is a consequence of, song.

Here – since her main domain was the Tagore song – she was going against the grain. Whatever Tagore intended for his interpreters, Rabindrasangeet, or the Tagore song, had, by the sixties, become a vehicle for bour-geois self-expression. By this I mean a humanism that places the self at the centre. Parodic self-expression is what became identifiable as emotion – darad or bhaab – in the Tagore song, and is almost all that remains of it today. The process began with three of the most popular exponents of the genre: Suchitra Mitra, Kanika Bandhyopadhyay, and Hemanta Mukherjee. Their earli-est recordings are memorable for their vitality. Things start to change in the mid-sixties, until their renditions come to occupy a middlebrow register, marked by cer-tain techniques and mannerisms: vibrato in Suchitra and Hemanta, leading to a portentous tremulousness; an exaggeration of meend, by all three, once more to simulate emotion. These mannerisms were then picked up by their various imitators, and used towards one end: to bring the self centre-stage. The project was also partly justified by the fact that Tagore was a poet, which implied that his words contained a meaning that had to be forcefully conveyed and dramatised.

228

Two artists took a different position: my mother, Bijoya Chaudhuri; and Subinoy Roy. My mother removed herself from the interpretation, putting the song centre-stage. The note must be allowed to speak for itself. Her convictions bring to mind Eliot's belief that 'emotion . . . has its life in the poem and not in the history' – implicit or explicit – 'of the poet'. Both her approach and Roy's to Rabindrasangeet were, I think, anti-humanist. The human must be set aside for the song to shine. Is this what Eliot meant when he said: 'Poetry . . . is not the expression of personality, but an escape from personality'? The refusal to give self or emotion centrality gives Roy's singing, and my mother's, a consistent calm. It also places them at an angle to their contemporaries.

Calm came, in terms of technique, from a rejection of vibrato, which is also hardly used in North Indian classical music. Though my mother never learnt classical music formally, she practised its techniques to the end of her life, and – though she didn't spend a huge amount of time listening to it till I began to sing khayal – was close to it temperamentally. Subinoy Roy was an admirer of Ustad Amir Khan. The Indian classical musical traditions are non-humanistic, in that their focus is not personality or psychology, but sur and taal, pitch and temporality. Vibrato adds emotion; but the note alone is joyous and equanimous, and makes the artist (and vibrato) redundant. The belief in the proximity of calm to joy goes back,

in India, at the very least to the tenth-century philosopher Abhinavagupta, who was also a theorist of rasa,
or aesthetic 'juice' or 'savouring'. There are nine rasas,
and, for Abhinavagupta, the one underlying them all –
the 'shant' or 'tranquil' rasa – is coeval with 'ananda',
'joy'. This is to point to a lineage also for a great deal
in nineteenth- and twentieth-century Western art that
constitutes a silent rebellion against the Enlightenment's
human-centred universe and its tendency to think of
art primarily as self-expression. Take Wordsworth's
curious remark that poetry is 'emotion recollected in
tranquillity'. How can emotion, felt or remembered,
be tranquil, unless by 'recollection' Wordsworth means
self-extinction?

There were two other ways in which my mother made the
musical note more important than herself. The first had to
do with her precision in pitching. Precision is often associated with control and objectivity, a privileging of fact
over embellishment. But precision also has a very long
history in many cultures – think of the haiku – related to
another sort of ambition. It means refusing to add, or to
supply, meaning, because the detail is significant already.
If there's craft involved in precision, it's to do with cur-
tailing the self's interference with what we hear and see.

Tagore, in his memoir *Jiban Smriti*, says that the first
rhyme he was drawn to as a child was the four-word
Bengali couplet *jal pade / pata nade* – 'The water falls, /

the leaf trembles'. On one level, this is indistinguishable from empirical detail; on another, it's an inaugural registering of the world's movement. Nothing has been added.

When the self empties itself, it becomes the world. It no longer needs to tell us of its feelings about a colour or object – it becomes colour; it becomes object. So Tagore, in the first verse of a poem called 'Ami', or 'Myself':

It's the colour of my consciousness that's made
    the emerald green,
        the ruby has become red.
I looked up at the sky:
    light began to shine
        in the east and west,
Turning to the rose, I said, 'Beautiful,'
    beautiful it became.
You'll say, This is information,
        not a poet's words.
I'll say, It's truth,
    that is why it's poetry.
This is *my* pride;
    – we all have a pride of our own.
                  (my translation)

The difference between objective fact ('information') and poetry isn't that the latter adds something to fact. It both surrenders to and creates what's true: the 'fact' that the rose is a rose, and that it's beautiful. For many, this isn't enough; they want a description of the rose's beauty. For Tagore, adding takes away from the transformative power of immersion: 'It's the colour of my consciousness that's made the emerald green.' As emotion and psychology recede, a consciousness of colour and beauty begin to emerge. The belief that this is possible he calls 'pride': an indifference, a hauteur, that also characterised my mother's investment in melody. Her voice is not imbued with emotion: it aims to become the music in the note – the emerald's green.

The other means by which my mother made room for the note is connected to a fundamental of Hindustani classical vocal music: aakar. The term refers to the cultivation of the 'ah' sound in meend and in alaap. The 'ah' liberates the self, dissolves it; the self's place is occupied by the note.

There's a tendency in Anglophone society to associate the 'aw' and 'oh' sounds with socialisation, politeness, civility. The 'ah', in comparison, is unbridled. It must be contained. You could see *My Fair Lady* as a sociospiritual allegory, where destiny and music are shaped by pivotal vowel sounds. It's possible to watch the opening scenes of the Broadway version on YouTube, where Julie Andrews is selling flowers in a square. She's still without self-consciousness – about who she is, about the social registers of the English language. She's poor and

unconstrained. As a prelude to singing, she makes gut-
tural vowel-based noises: 'Aaau! Aaaau! Aaaaau!' Then,
with some tradesmen keeping the chorus, she starts to
sing a song about losing oneself in a reverie: 'Wouldn't It
Be Loverly', a daydream of idleness, satiety, and warmth.

> All I want is a room somewhere
> Far away from the cold night air
> With one enormous chair
> Ah wouldn't it be loverly?

The opening vowel – in 'All' – is attenuated; but the
Cockney mouth opens wider and wider with 'some-
where', 'far', 'away', 'air', 'chair', and even 'lah-verly'.
The words are both apposite and redundant; we feel
the presence of pure voice, especially in the impassioned
'Ah' before each 'Wouldn't it be loverly'.

This 'ah', or 'aakar', is subsequently corseted and
tamed. The story of *My Fair Lady* is the story of how
happiness must be found in gentility; how what's
unbounded must be checked. By the time Julie Andrews
sings 'I Could Have Danced All Night', the polite self
is firmly in place: 'dance' verges on 'dawnce'; the singing is tremulous. It has emotion, underlined by a light
vibrato, but – although it's a song expressing Eliza
Doolittle's new-found joy in love – the flower-seller's
self-forgetfulness has gone. As has the 'ah'.

*

The pop-rock artist who most courted self-extinction in singing was John Lennon. In no other performer in that genre do we hear such gasps and 'ah' sounds. The singing itself is reed-thin, pure, as in 'Lucy in the Sky with Diamonds': melody on oblivion's brink. Here's a singer who barely chooses to exist. The great self-expunging 'aahs' occur in 'A Day in the Life'. After the bodiless vocalising of the first section, there's a mild waviness, a shruti, at its end, in the words 'turn you on': a sign of oncoming dissolution. An alarm clock goes off. Routine asserts itself with McCartney – 'woke up, fell out of bed' – matter-of-fact, worldly. Soon, however, Lennon's 'aahs' take over, returning us to the dream-state.

Lennon's 'aahs' can be heard in recordings prior and subsequent to 'A Day in the Life'. They punctuate his idea of song, and give to his singing (which could be melodiously raucous, as in 'Twist and Shout') a never-worked-up laziness: a teetering towards escape from the fatigue of being. It's there in the early 'A Hard Day's Night', starting with the 'ah' in the word 'hard', in the evenness of the singing – a kind of rock samadhi whose unexcitability is clearer in contrast to McCartney's pressing 'When I'm home' – and in the drowsy 'mmm' with which Lennon returns, after the interjection, to the prospect of retreating from daytime consciousness. It's neither sex nor sleep he wants.

The other 'aahs' I love include the one before the third chorus in 'Ticket to Ride', where the self swoons forgetfully in the midst of the complaint; and the 'aahs' in 'Because' and 'Sun King' on *Abbey Road*. The singer is so recumbent – there's an in-breathing hiss before the words 'sun king' are sung – that he can hardly animate himself: both songs, very short, are bursts of breath.

The calm of Lennon's style comes from detachment. In some Beatles songs, his lines represent a departure from emotion that's being played out elsewhere: for instance, the tranquil 'Everybody had a hard year / everybody had a good time' at the end of 'I've Got a Feeling', a song that's mainly a showcase for McCartney's robust rock vocals. Lennon is both in the song and strangely, wonderfully indifferent.

The great anti-humanist development in modern Western song comes with the blues. We know it's an expression of human – specifically, African American – anguish. But two things won't let it be pinned down to the humanistic. The first is the blues' pentatonic scale. The second is the relative eschewal of vibrato, and blues' singing's 'ah'-based sound.

The pentatonic is a scale found worldwide in several variants. The blues is its modern African American incarnation, and comprises a departure from the mimesis of post-Enlightenment Western music, in which the major seven-note scale is happy, the minor sad. The pentatonic fits into neither one side nor the other in this binary. It shapes the blues, but also lends itself to the high spirits of rock and roll, the pounding ecstasy of rock. It generates an experience beyond happy–sad. The role of the blues may be to communicate pain, but the pentatonic embodies pure life and aliveness. So the blues becomes radiant; it becomes – without in any humanistic or Christian sense being 'positive' or 'uplifting' – joyous.

The joyousness finds voice in the singing, a vocalising with no antecedents in opera, plainsong, evensong, or in white renditions of swing music, where there's a tendency to constrict the mouth and vowel, and add, according to context, vibrato. Compare Fred Astaire's 'Cheek to Cheek', where the singing is light, charming, 'o'-based, bordering on falsetto, with Ella Fitzgerald and Louis Armstrong's version, where the mouth is open, and there's no vibrato except what's organic to their voices. The latter's singing descends from the blues style, where note is given precedence over singer. Its first great recorded practitioner is maybe Bessie Smith. The southern origins of these singers means that certain key words – like 'I' – open up into 'ah'. The home of the self, the 'I', becomes, in Smith, the 'ah' of the musical note.

The Tagore song (Rabindrasangeet) is probably the first expression of a pure middle-class sensibility in Bengal; maybe even in India. It and the bhadralok – literally, in Bengali, 'polite people' – belong to each other. In it, Tagore created, between 1878 (when he was seventeen) and his death in 1941, a deceptively simple (by the standards of Indian classical music) genre of extraordinary subtlety and variety of register, bringing to his words a finesse, sensuousness, and philosophical beauty that it's hardly ever the song's role, or ambition, to achieve.

Rabindrasangeet and its interpretation are the site of a contest between modernist and anti-humanist impulses on the one hand and human-centred self-expression on the other. There are deep reserves of calm in the Tagore song, tapped by singers like Subinoy Roy. But Roy is an exception; the Tagore song, over decades, was seized by politeness, and an accentuation, in the careers of Suchitra Mitra and Kanika Bandhyopadhyay, of the 'aw' sound. The 'aw' sound in Bengali speech denominated class and socialisation. It's not to be found in aakar-based khayal singing, and can't be compared with the 'o' in the non-sense 'nom tom' syllables of dhrupad, which have no associations of class.

Early exponents of Rabindrasangeet, like Kanak Das and K. L. Saigal, who recorded in the thirties and forties, owe much to the classical temperament. Their renditions – whatever the emotional content of the words – are 'ah'-based, self-forgetful, and joyous. What's audible in their recordings is purity of tone, and the fact that singing is a kind of freedom. The ponderousness, the careful politeness are a few decades away.

Having noted the secular Bengali, and Indian, middle class's ambivalence towards classical music – because

of its social milieu, but also because of what was mis-
understood as religious content – it should also be
said that the resurrection of the classical arts in India
owes a lot to this middle class, especially in the early
to mid-twentieth century: to its receptivity and patronage. Actual crossovers from the middle class to the field
of classical practice are rare, but not unheard of: take,
for instance, the sitar player Ravi Shankar, the son of a
barrister. In comparison to the reconstruction of monu-
ments and archaeological sites, which is the result of a
collaboration between colonials and Indians, the revival
of the classical traditions in music and dance is entirely a
consequence of a partnership between traditional practitioners and Indian moderns. The English found these
forms utterly alien. The response of the late-nineteenth-
and twentieth-century Indian modern to classical music
and classical texts is modernist, secular, and aesthetic,
rather than utopian, proprietary, and reverential. This
revolutionary engagement with antiquity and classicism
might be one reason why Western classical music never
gained centrality in India.

Aakar in singing – and, alongside it, the abjuring of emotion and vibrato – is accompanied by calm (shanti) and joy
(ananda). This insight emerges from a creative and critical tradition in India which contributes to developments
in Europe from the late eighteenth century and early
nineteenth century onwards, when Hindu and Buddhist

texts begin to become available in European languages, and, suddenly, theories of 'disinterestedness' and 'impersonality' start to abound among Western philosophers, poets, critics, and novelists.

It's the *Gita* (circa second to fifth century BCE) that's possibly the earliest text to articulate the notion that an act may be passionate and detached at once; in other words, involve both the expression and the annulment of the self. Krishna, addressing Arjuna, who's despondent on the eve of going to war with his cousins, instructs him in a peculiar definition of action:

Set thy heart upon thy work, but never on its reward.
Work not for a reward; but never cease to do thy work.
  Do thy work in the peace of Yoga and, free from
selfish desires, be not moved in success or in failure. Yoga
is evenness of mind – a peace that is ever the same.
                                    (trans. Juan Mascaro)

The *Gita*'s impact in the West, where Charles Wilkins' English translation becomes available in 1785, and the French in 1787, is most palpable in the realm of the aesthetic. Kant, in 1790, in the *Critique of Judgment*, arrives at his formulation that aesthetic experience constitutes a form of 'disinterestedness'; the pleasure it gives is unconnected to the satisfaction of desire. Creativity he describes as 'purposeful purposelessness'. These observations have few forebears in European thought, but

239

have a very long lineage in the Indian texts that had then just begun to circulate in Europe.

In 1865, Matthew Arnold, without mentioning Kant, uses the word 'disinterested' not of creative but of critical work, which he sees as neither subjective nor objective assessment, but as calm, detached 'action'. Without naming it, he makes a reference, in his essay 'The Function of Criticism at the Present Time', to the *Gita*, which he'd begun to study in 1845.

> It will be said that it is a very subtle and indirect
> action which I am thus prescribing for criticism and
> that, by embracing in this manner the Indian virtue of
> detachment and abandoning the sphere of practical life,
> it condemns itself to a slow and obscure work. Slow
> and obscure it may be, but it is the only proper work of
> criticism.

With Kant in relation to creativity, and then with Arnold in relation to critical thought, we see a gradual abandoning of the idea that it's the writer's or the artist's job to express themselves through emotion or opinion.

The most significant Western theorist of literary craft, roughly contemporary with Arnold and preceding Eliot, is Flaubert, Joyce's mentor. Flaubert was immersed in Buddhist texts and, by the time he began writing *Madame Bovary*, was convinced that 'reality' couldn't be constructed artificially in fiction, but must be arrived at or discovered through authorial surrender. Word and detail must gain precedence, and author become secondary. In 1852, Flaubert writes to Louise Colet: 'I don't believe you have any idea what kind of book this one is . . . No lyricism, no reflections, the personality of the author absent.' Also: 'the author in his work must be like God in the universe, present everywhere and visible nowhere'. What sort of deity does Flaubert have in mind when he refers to an author–creator who brings the work to life by withdrawing from it? The Christian God is either an overseer up above, or a paternal creator who sends a temporary emissary, a progeny, to earth. For the contradictory being Flaubert describes as a model – who's simultaneously invested in, and detached from, creation – we have to look at the opening verses of the *Isa Upanishad*: 'He moves, and he moves not. He is far, and he is near. He is within all, and he is outside all.' (By 1796, the Frenchman Abraham Hyacinthe Anquetil Duperron had translated fifty Upanishads from Persian translations into Latin.)

The paradox of detachment starts establishing the foundations, by the end of the nineteenth century, for the curious yoga of 'modernism'.

In 'Lapis Lazuli', we have a striking instance of an Anglophone poet, W. B. Yeats, arguing for the ananda that accompanies calm. His word for it is 'gaiety'.

All perform their tragic play,
There struts Hamlet, there is Lear,
That's Ophelia, that Cordelia;
Yet they, should the last scene be there,
The great stage curtain about to drop,
If worthy their prominent part in the play,
Do not break up their lines to weep.
They know that Hamlet and Lear are gay;
Gaiety transfiguring all that dread.

Yeats is reminding us – as he often did, but from yet another perspective this time – of art's difference from life. We exude our tragic losses; actors are both invested in and detached from theirs: 'they . . . / Do not break up their lines to weep'. Is there a meeting-point, here, between ananda and 'catharsis', what Aristotle called the 'pleasure' of the tragic, and the 'purgation', in the audience, of 'pity and fear'? To a point. Aristotle is focused on the peculiar way in which we receive tragedy. Yeats focuses on the artist: the fact that the artist experiences a detached joy *only* in becoming Hamlet or Lear: 'Gaiety transfiguring all that dread'.

This has a bearing on the decisions that made my mother refuse, unlike some other exponents of the Tagore song, to 'break up [her] lines to weep'.

4
'Mishearing'

If I'm not mistaken, there's a story or an essay by F. Scott Fitzgerald about a man emerging from twenty years of alcoholism, noticing the city he lives in as if for the first time, and blinking at the sunlight. I may have made up some of the details in my head, but I think of this story and Fitzgerald when I take into account my return, after sixteen years of denying pop, to my old record collection.

Of course, Hindustani classical music wasn't an illness, and I won't need to 'recover' from it. It was more a religious conversion. Not a superficial conversion, but one entailing a new regime and way of looking at the world, and, at first, a sense of 'rightness' and homecoming. This last gives the convert a zeal that goes beyond dedication to an art: a new-found authenticity, and a rejection of the past. So I began to feel, when I was seventeen or eighteen (although I was still composing songs on the guitar): 'This is *my* music. It's related to this light, these sounds. I neither knew this music before, nor really listened to these sounds nor saw this light.'

I can date the Fitzgeraldian period more or less exactly because it began when I travelled to London in September 1983, leaving my guitar behind and carrying a small tanpura. It ended in May 1999, when I came back to India. So, around sixteen years. By then, the convert's zeal had receded: it became something to be studied in retrospect with wonder and amusement. In Calcutta, my wife, daughter (eight months old), and I joined my parents. It was the last days of hi-fi systems; we knew they were scarce, but not that their reign was over. There was a Videocon hi-fi in the drawing room which wasn't working. In anticipation of our return, my father got it repaired by a technician who had no fixed address, but did his job under a tree. My father never saw him again. The thing started to function, and I – having made peace with my teenage years – began once again to play Crosby, Stills and Nash, Deep Purple, and even *Jesus Christ Superstar*. I allowed myself to take pleasure without suspicion.

It was while listening in 2004 to a posthumously released selection of Jimi Hendrix's blues-based recordings that I realised that the blues scale was identical to ragas like Jog, Dhani, and Malkauns. What they had in common was the minor pentatonic, whose notes, besides the tonic, include the flat third, the fourth, the fifth, and the flat seventh. I should have noticed this twenty years earlier, when I'd begun to learn Hindustani classical music. Certain congruences are so plain that you tend not to spot them, and maybe it was the passage of time that made the echo of the one in the other audible. I began to listen to the Jimi Hendrix recordings – to the blues scale in particular – with a special sense of discovery, with

246

the sort of surprise you feel when, with a puzzle, you see a pattern resembling first one thing, and, the next moment, something else.

Very soon, I named this 'double hearing', which sounds like a disorder, but which I meant as an acknowledgement of becoming aware, unexpectedly, that I was standing at the confluence of something. 'Double hearing' came to me early in the new millennium, alongside my decision to be no longer shackled to the novel, to test other forms, to give the short story and essay a try, to spend much of my time at home, to be a father, to familiarise myself with the new India.

Soon – a week – after listening to those Hendrix recordings, I had a moment of 'mishearing'. For decades, I have, every morning, sung one raga: Gujri Todi. I'm never bored of it: it's like a familiar walk which somehow never repeats itself. That morning, I felt disoriented at one point. Some of the notes I'd sung – <u>dha</u> má <u>dha</u> ni <u>dha</u> má <u>dha</u> – reminded me of the riff to 'Layla'. I reported this to my wife. The 'mishearing' had caught me unawares, but my 'double hearing' – the renewed attention I'd been paying to the blues scale – must have led up to it. Gujri Todi has six notes, sa <u>re</u> <u>ga</u> má <u>dha</u> ni, but, if you ignore the sa, as you occasionally do, you're elaborating on a blues pentatonic. 'Do you think this – Todi leading to "Layla" – is a convincing basis for a composition, or an experiment?' I asked her.

*

Two weeks later, I was still having 'mishearings'. My wife, mother, and I, and possibly my daughter, went to investigate the opening of a new hotel, the ITC Sonar Bangla, on the EMS Bypass – a bit of highway that had no prior existence for us. A mad family expedition. We went in, immersed ourselves in luxury, critiqued it (how quickly wealth palls!), emerging almost immediately. The santoor was playing in the lobby. Why does the santoor's steely melodiousness have an afterlife in hotels? Naturally, I blocked out the sound. Then, waiting for the car to come up the driveway, I found myself listening. The santoor was playing 'Auld Lang Syne'. No, it wasn't – it was raga Pahadi, based on the major pentatonic that many folk melodies owe their form to. 'Pahadi' means 'of the hills'; isn't 'Auld Lang Syne' a Highlands tune?

These convergences didn't instruct me that music is a universal language. To create a universal language, you must be comfortable with the idea that the elements that add up to that universality – specific cultures, languages, and traditions which are putatively part of a great family – have a recognisability and integrity. But my 'mishearings' – of Todi becoming the riff to 'Layla'; of Pahadi becoming 'Auld Lang Syne' – implied an unravelling. My subconscious could have been alert to these correspondences only because it had had its seed-time

in metropolitan sixties and seventies Bombay, in a kind
of sensory hum arising from The Who and Hindi film
music and car horns and my mother's Tagore songs and
Joni Mitchell and Kishori Amonkar and sea breeze. I
couldn't be aware of all these elements chronologically
or encyclopaedically, as a sum total of my 'Indianness'.
I could only be made newly conscious of them through
accident, which is what 'mishearing' is. It didn't affirm
my identity; it reminded me that I know, and have listened to, more than I think I have.

Late in 2004, I began to approach musicians in Calcutta
with a rock and jazz background to work through these
ideas. Subsequently, 'The "Layla" Riff to Todi' came into
being. Then, unprompted, other opportunities presented
themselves.

In Park Street one afternoon, I wondered if All India
Radio's beautiful theme tune could be relocated in a harmonic setting and improvised upon. Not in Shivaranjani,
the raga it had been composed in, but a version I'd made
up, in raga Marwa. By now, All India Radio is obso-
lete; hardly anyone I know listens to it. Its theme will
survive it – as a haunting example of what a clarion
call to the nation sounded like. My repertoire of 'mishearings' grew. The musicians I'd brought together and
I decided to do a concert in January 2005. The last song
I wrote before the performance was 'Trucker', based on
the legend on the backs of trucks on Indian highways:

'buri nazar wale tera muh kala' – 'May your face be blackened, you with the evil eye.'

Each one of these pieces felt like a bad idea. Each time, as I did after confiding my first 'mishearing' to my wife, I took the plunge. In fact, I can't recall when I've thought that anything I was about to do – novel, poem, or composition – was a sensible undertaking.

'What do I call it?' I asked my wife, because the invitation cards were to be printed. 'Because whatever else it is, it's not fusion.' 'Then call it that,' she said. 'What?' '"This Is Not Fusion".'

I went to Berlin in the autumn of 2005, to spend five months there – my first time away from home after we'd returned to India in 1999. I was very taken with the city's grid of streets and U-Bahn lines in which history often intersected with the present. Knowing almost no German, I became peculiarly attuned. To not understand the language of a place you're visiting for three days is customary; to understand little during five months leads to your ear listening not for meaning but rises and falls in pitch, intonations and inflections. Whenever I took the U-Bahn from Krumme Lanke to Freie Universität or Wittenbergplatz, I noted a succession of sounds in the seconds between the train's arrival and its departure: a vibration as it waited, a bass note; a voice that said

'Einsteigen bitte' as I entered, words that had no meaning for me but which I obeyed; the same voice saying 'Zurückbleiben bitte', followed by a signal made up of two repeated notes before the doors closed, the notes comprising the fourth and fifth in relation to the train's vibration; then a kind of sigh, as the train started, that covered an octave. Day after day, I listened closely, partly because it was only I who heard the sounds, which had no significance to others; and to check if they varied from train to train.

From these sounds I made a song called 'Berlin'. When I went back to Calcutta for Christmas, I discussed the vibration, the octave-long sigh, the cautionary fourth and fifth with a keyboard player, and, alongside the chords I'd set the song to, put a track in place.

In January or February, my last months in Berlin, I saw a thin man get into the U-Bahn and pitch his copies of *Motz* (a paper sold by the homeless) to bored commuters. My knowledge of German hadn't improved since September; I passively noted his voice's sing-song. It reminded me of something – a faraway tune, upbeat, nonsensical, something which I'd encountered before and at once crossed the road to avoid. Both the man's speech (whose meaning I could guess at) and his forlorn delivery led me to think up a tune, a musical ambience, and the words:

Thank you for listening kindly
And sparing me a second.
I know you're sitting blindly
And thinking of the weekend.
I sell a paper called *Motz*,
It really is a treasure.
I live not far from Ostkreuz,
I'm not a man of leisure.

My melody echoed a tune whose name I didn't know; later, I found out it was the first bar of the Vengaboys' 'We Like to Party' that the homeless man had unwittingly conjured up. I added three verses, and opted for a disco setting: disco, which, at the end of the seventies, had made me give up on pop music.

One thing I've felt again and again in the course of this project is that all music – whether it's a rock riff or a snatch of melody from some loathed genre – is sound, and has an independent life among the sounds one has heard and forgotten; and that all sound – a tramp's voice; the hum in a machine – is music. We navigate this doubleness. When the moment comes, familiar notes become sound, or a familiar sound becomes a note.

I had begun to listen to the music of my environment in my gap year in St Cyril Road, when Girdharji would ask me to measure the kulfi seller's bell against the tonic of the raga I was practising.

As Bharata said, music starts in the cattle lowing; the peacock's cry. There are hardly any pre-existing nota-tions as far as Indians are concerned. Both Amir Khusro from the thirteenth century and Naushad, one of the first major 'music directors' in Hindi cinema, disavowed the idea of the composer: 'Say, instead,' said Naushad, 'that it was this land that created these songs.'

Acknowledgements

I'd like to thank Alex Bowler and Edwin Frank for their close reading of the MS; Meru Gokhale and Shiny Das for their swift responses and support; Jill Burrows, music editor, for her very useful suggestions; Emmie Francis and Anne Owen for help with various things; and Michael Downes for his splendid copy-editing. Kajal Basu did some meticulous fact-checking, for which I thank him here.

I am grateful to Katherine Schofield for going through the MS carefully at very short notice. Those who are interested in the history of the khayal should look towards her contributions. In this context, I should thank Aneesh Pradhan for introducing me to Katherine. I also thank the music critic Meena Banerjee for being receptive to my queries.

Susan Leslie Boynton, Professor of Music and Historical Musicology at Columbia University, read the MS too. I was lucky to get to know her during my nine months in Paris as a fellow at the Columbia Institute of Ideas and Imagination. It was there that I also met the composer Zosha de Castri, another fellow, with whom I discussed some of these ideas, as I did with the

Paris-based pianist John Kamfonas. I thank them all for their patience and generosity. Much of this book was written during that fellowship in Paris, in a flat on rue de Poissonniers.

The original of the painting by Bulaki reproduced in the book can be found in the Mehrangarh Museum.

My agent Sarah Chalfant and her colleague Alba Ziegler-Bailey have become a bit like family, and have looked out for this book as they have for me. My wife has long been a bit like my literary editor and agent, available at most times of the day and night for advice. Both she and my daughter Aruna have shown great patience over the years during my long practice sessions.

A Selection of Works Referred to in the Text

Roland Barthes, *Mythologies*, Vintage, 2009

J. M. Coetzee, *Stranger Shores: Literary Essays,
1986–1999*, Penguin, 2001

Bob Dylan: 'Don't Think Twice, It's All Right', written
by Bob Dylan; © 1963 by Warner Bros. Inc.; renewed
1991 by Special Rider Music. 'It Ain't Me Babe',
written by Bob Dylan; © 1964 by Warner Bros. Inc.;
renewed 1992 by Special Rider Music. 'Idiot Wind',
written by Bob Dylan; © 1974 by Ram's Horn
Music; renewed 2002 by Ram's Horn Music

T. S. Eliot, *Selected Essays*, Faber and Faber, 1999

E. M. Forster, *Howards End*, Edward Arnold, 1910

Philip Larkin, extract taken from 'Days' © Estate
of Philip Larkin; first appeared in *The Whitsun
Weddings*, 1964. Reprinted by permission of Faber
& Faber Ltd

John Lennon/Paul McCartney, 'I've Got a Feeling'
© Sony/ATV Music Publishing LLC

Alan Jay Lerner and Frederick Loewe, 'Wouldn't It Be
Loverly', 1956 © Warner Chappell Music, Inc.

A SELECTION OF WORKS REFERRED TO IN THE TEXT

Robert Lowell, 'from Brunetto Latini' (Canto XV of
Dante's *Inferno*), *Collected Poems*, Farrar, Straus,
and Giroux, 2000
Thomas Mann, *Death in Venice (Tristan. Tonio
Kroeger)*, Penguin, 1955
Satyajit Ray, *Our Films, Their Films*, Orient
BlackSwan, 1976
Rabindranath Tagore, *Letters from a Young Poet
1887–1895* (trans. Rosinka Chaudhuri), Penguin,
2014

AMIT CHAUDHURI is the author of seven novels, including, most recently, *Friend of My Youth*. Among his other published works are collections of short stories, poetry, and essays, as well as the nonfiction *Calcutta* and a critical study of D. H. Lawrence's poetry. He has received the Commonwealth Writers Prize, the Betty Trask Award, the Encore Prize, the Los Angeles Times Book Prize, and the Sahitya Akademi Award, among other accolades. Chaudhuri is a Fellow of the Royal Society of Literature and holds the titles of Professor of Contemporary Literature at the University of East Anglia in England and Professor of Creative Writing at Ashoka University in India. In addition, he is a singer in the North Indian classical tradition and a composer and performer in a project that brings together the raga, blues, and jazz with a variety of other musical traditions. In 2017 he received the Sangeet Samman from the government of West Bengal for his contribution to Indian classical music. Chaudhuri's music has been regularly featured on radio and television; his version of "Summertime" was featured on the BBC 4 documentary *Gershwin's Summertime: The Song That Conquered the World*.